Mortality Schedule
of the
Eastern Shore
of
Maryland
1870

ಐಐಐಐ

Janet Wilson Riley

Heritage Books
2025

HERITAGE BOOKS

AN IMPRINT OF HERITAGE BOOKS, INC.

Books, CDs, and more—Worldwide

For our listing of thousands of titles see our website
at
www.HeritageBooks.com

A Facsimile Reprint
Published 2025 by
HERITAGE BOOKS, INC.
Publishing Division
5810 Ruatan Street
Berwyn Heights, MD 20740

International Standard Book Number
Paperbound: 978-0-7884-3053-4

To My Sons,

Darius W. Riley Jr
Richard D. Riley

This one is for you
With Love.

A special thanks to Darius, Debby, and Deanna again

JWR 1985

KEY

NAME   AGE/SEX   MONTH DIED   CAUSE of DEATH

8	PEOPLES George	11/12	(pfb) Jan	measles
9	BURK Rebecca	40 m	(Ir) Apr Keeping house	puerperal fever
157	DAVIS Jane	72 (w)	May	paralysis
223	THOMAS Mary	25B m	Apr Keeping house	pneumonia
367	_____ _____	(f)	Oct	cholera infantum
3--	_____ _____	(m)63 (m)	Jul	inflammation bowel
66	HENRY Harriet	3/12	Feb	unknown

HOUSEHOLD
NUMBER

MARRIED/
WIDOWED

PLACE
OF
BIRTH

OCCUPATION

PARENTS FOREIGN BORN (pfb)
MOTHER FOREIGN BORN (mfb)
FATHER FOREIGN BORN (ffb)

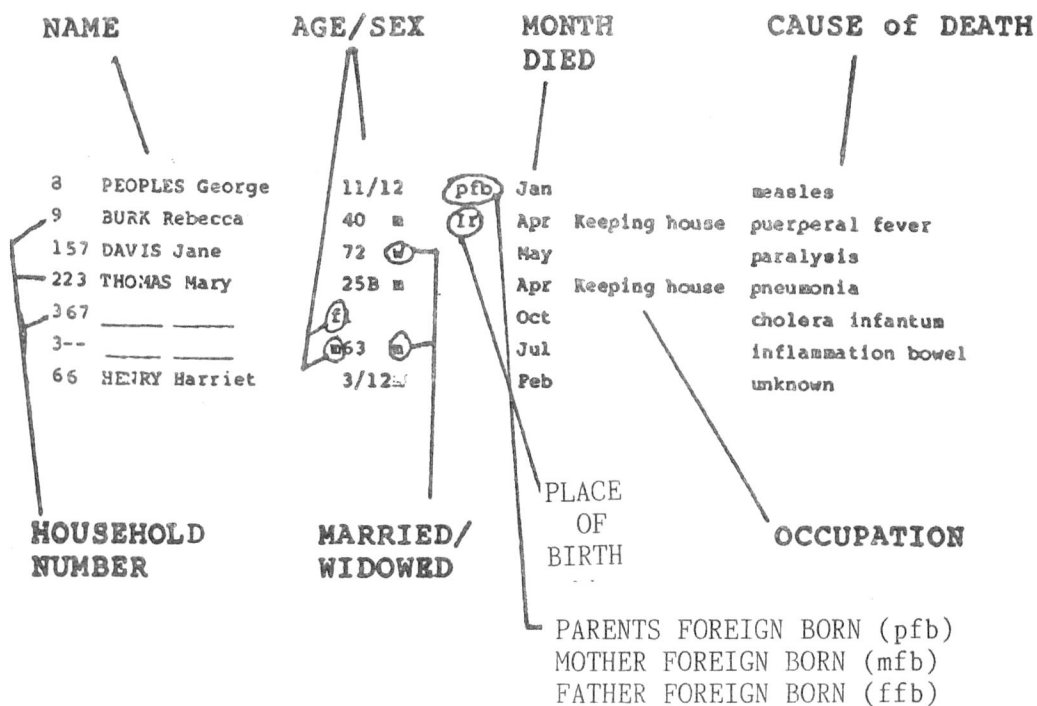

ABBREVIATIONS FOR PLACE OF BIRTH

Al	Alabama	Ma	Massachusettes
		Me	Maine
Ba	Bavaria	Mi	Mississippi
Bar	Barbadoes		
Bd	Baden	NC	North Carolina
		NH	New Hampshire
Ch	China	NJ	New Jersey
Ct	Connecticut	NY	New York
DC	District of Columbia	OH	Ohio
De	Delaware		
		Pa	Pennsylvania
En	England	Pr	Prussia
Fl	Florida	SC	South Carolina
Fr	France	Sct	Scotland
		SL	St Louis
Ge	Germany		
Gu	Guianea	Tn	Tennessee
Ha	Hanover	Va	Virginia
HC	Hesse Cassel	Vt	Vermont
Ia	Indiana	Wa	Washington
Il	Illinois	Wi	Wisconsin
Ir	Ireland		
Ka	Kansas		
Ky	Kentucky		

INTRODUCTION

Mortality schedules exist for the census years 1850, 1860, 1870, and 1880. Enumerators were required to keep a list of all persons in each district who had died since the 31st of May of the previous year.

These schedules provide much information to genealogists, historians and statisticians alike. Each schedule identifies the household to which the individual belonged (in most cases), age, sex, race, marital status, occupation, month deceased, place of birth, cause of death as well as length of illness. This data is invaluable in an era when vital statistics were poorly, if at all, recorded.

In the couse of bureaucratic time, it was decided that these records were of no value and were scheduled for destruction. Th DAR sought to prevent this. The Mortality Schedules were given in 1918 and 1919 to the respective states and placed in non-federal repositories. Maryland's schedules are in the possession of the State Library in Annapolis.

This volume is an effort to make this valuable data more available to the public. Vital records for the State of Maryland were not kept until 1898 except for the City of Baltimore which are extant since 1875. Scattered records exist in some of the Eastern Shore counties prior to this time. Parish records also contain some vital records for their parishioners. This work is far from comprehensive but it does provide an additional resource to genealogists and researchers interested in the Eastern Shore of Maryland.

Janet Wilson Riley
Toms River, NJ
1985

11	LAMBERT Mary	1/12B		May		consumption
2	KEMP Richard	73		Apr		dropsey
6	CARLISLE Charles	1/12		Sep		croup
44	CLARK Sallie	2	De	Jul		whooping cough
67	SHERWOOD Margaret	50		Jul		consumption
194	LEWIS Clinton	2		Dec		typhoid
137	DOWNS Benjamin	19		Jan		accidently shot self
	_____ Louisa	76 m		Apr	Keeping house	apoplexy
29	BERRY Cornella	55B m		May	Keeping house	consumption
29	WILKERSON Robert	8B		Sep		paralysis
38	WILSON Robert	25		Aug	Clerk	dropsey
297	LUCAS Samuel H	11/12		Dec		brain fever
219	STRAUGHN Thomas	73 m		Oct	Minister	paralysis
226	MILLER Sarah M	32		Nov		consumption
76	BANTUM Adaline	43B w		Mch		consumption
146	BELL Maggie	10/12		Oct		measles
188	GREEN Eliza	B m		Aug		disease of liver
193	McNAMARA James	3		May		pneumonia
198	RUSSAM Rhoda	38 m		Jan		pneumonia
198	OUTEN James Fletcher	?/12	De	Mch		consumption
206	C_____ Henrietta	31B m		Sep		unknown
	_____ _____	f22 m		Dec		whooping cough
269	SLAUGHTER Isabel	f3	De	Jan		consumption
280	_____ Henrietta	31B m		Jul		dysentary
280	Mary	45		Dec		consumption
286	PEARSON	f26		Dec		cancer of liver
9	DRAPER Margaret A	34 m		Feb		pneumonia
29	CONNOLLY Amy A	28 m	De	Dec		childbirth
30	BROWN EDW Constantine	30		Dec	Captain	consumption
94	GADD Mary C	32 m		Aug		consumption
110	TURNER Laura Euphemia	1		Aug		cholera infantum
125	McFARLAND Charlotte	33 m	En	Mch		typhoid fever
127	MANSFIELD Mary V	9/12		May		whooping cough
-	SELBY Laura A	15		Mch		liver disease
-	WILSON Florence	9/12		Jul		croup
185		ml		Feb		whooping cough
193	WILLIAMS Susan Ella	1		Feb		pneumonia
2	E SON Elizabeth R	1	NJ	Oct		cholera infantum
2	E SON M ___ Julian	7/12	NJ	Jan		cholera infantum
4	DOWNS Raymond Wm	8/12		Sep		cholera infantum
21	TURNER James	6/12B		Jan		whooping cough
27	SMITH Mary Florence	2		Jul		whooping cough
27	SMITH Henry A	43 m		Aug		falling body
197	BLOCKSON David	43 m	De	Aug	Lawyer	inflammation bowels
260	WILLIAMS Wm A	35 m		Jan	Farmer	consumption
291	HUGH Walter	36 m		Feb	Farmer	pneumonia

-1-

292	ELLWANGER Hartley	3-	m	Ger	Oct	Farmer	intermittant fever
333	_____ Enoch	43	m		Jan	Farmer	pneumonia
352	_____ Solomon	--	m		Apr	Farmer	apoplexy
363	DAVIS John	--B	m		May	Laborer	pneumonia
363	_____ Isaac	--B	m		Apr		pneumonia
399	WEBSTER Thomas	--	m	De	Aug	Farmer	consumption
410	____er Robert	--	m	De	Mch	Farmer	pleurisy
416	BELL _____	--B	m		Dec	Farmer	heart disease
422	W___ Louisa	33	m		Jan		consumption
*	EMERSON Sarah L	50	m		Mch		consumption

* Denton dist #3

DISTRICT #3 - CAROLINE COUNTY 1870

33	TOWNS George E	20		NH	Jul		epilepsy
34	EVETTS Ann	70			May		unknown
58	JOPP Edward	3/12		p/fb	Jul		cholera infantum
81	WOOD Martha	15			Apr		pneumonia
95	LANG Samuel	60	w		Dec	Farmer	consumption
112	KEMP John W	9/12			Mch		whooping cough
135	HUBBARD Mary	95	m		Mch	Keeping house	asthma
146	WOOTERS Tamzey	40	m		Aug	Keeping house	fever
150	TRICE Laura	2			Feb		whooping cough
190	MILLER Martha	7/12			Feb		whooping cough
191	GRIFFITH Ann W S	50	w		Jun		consumption
202	ARGO Charles	5/12			Jul		cholera infantum
28	SIMPSON Thomas P	45	m		Jan	Tailor	consumption

DISTRICT #4 -CAROLINE COUNTY 1870

5	COLLINS Abram G	57	m		Sep	Farmer	typhoid fever
20	WILLIS Henry	48			Nov	Farmer	consumption
39	DEEN Lacy	1			Aug		cholera infantum
92	WENTWORTH Esther	15		Me	Oct		typhoid fever
108	FRIEND James	75B	m		Sep	Farmer	consumption
127	BOWBY Mary	30B	m		Jun	Keeping house	consumption
131	CAUSEY Henrietta	9/12B			Jul		measles
185	RICH Charles W	8/12B			May		infant unknown
229	WHEELER Henrietta V	5/12			Feb		whooping cough
244	FRIEND Gabriel	80B	m		Jun	Farmer	typhoid fever
260	FLUHARTY William	38	m		Apr	Sailor	pneumonia
359	COULBORN Alverde	4/12			May		cholera infantum
368	SHARP Margaret	38B	w		Mch	Keeping house	consumption
407	STEVENS Wilbert W	2/12			Jun		cholera infantum
407	STEVENS Martha L	3/12			Jul		cholera infantum
449	PARKER John	55			Jun	Laborer	scrofula

DISTRICT #5 - CAROLINE COUNTY 1870

36	JAMES Anna C	17B		Jul	Domestic	pneumonia
44	JESTER Peter	68 m		Mch	Farmer	pneumonia
103	NICHOLS Henry	1/12		Mch		unknown
110	WILSON John	2	Pa	Jan		cerebro spinal fever
110	WILSON Anna	6	Pa	May		heart disease
111	CONNELLY Rebecca	84 w		Oct		neuralgia
113	BARNES George K	1/12		May		unknown
138	CONNELLY Britana	68 m		Aug	Keeping house	cancer
147	SULLIVAN Jacob	15		Feb	Farm laborer	diabetes
152	ANDREW Charles	48 m		May	Carpenter	consumption
168	SEDGWICK Sarah A	3	De	Jun		dysentary
164	SHEPPARD Adam	85B w		Jan		pneumonia
184	COOK Clara	6/12B		Feb		whooping cough
196	BOWDLE Daniel	50 m		Apr	Laborer	consumption
221	RICKETTS James	3/12B		Apr		unknown
224	CANNON Jane	12B		Sep		typhoid fever

3	McDANIEL George	32	m	De	May	Laborer	murdered
32	DOUGLAS Robert C	64B	m		Apr	Fisherman	drowned
41	BROWN James	73	m	IR	Dec	Farmer	gangrene
57	McNEAL Minnie T	2			Mch		mesenterica
77	GUTHRIE Geoegeanna	4/12			Mch		mesenterica
126	GRANT A Rebecca	1			Dec		cholera infantum
150	PALMER Keziah	80	w	De	Sep	lived with son	congestion of brain
175	LEMON Martha J	17			Jun		pertusis pulmonary
237	STILES Henry S	64	m	Pa	Mch	ret Farmer	pneumonia
270	WHIMBLE Nancy	80	w		Apr		pneumonia
289	JONES Mary M	37	m		Jan	Keeping House	cancer of stomach
289	JONES John B	2/12			Sep		mesenterica
291	GOODYEAR RB	m19		Pa	Jul	Baker	phthsis pulmonary
298	WOLF Mary A	25		De			phthsis pulmonary
303	THOMAS Benjamin	20B			Jan	Farm worker	phthsis pulmonary
319	FOSTER Marjary	77	m		Mch	Housekeeping	pneumonia
320	NORRIS Samuel	30	m	De	Apr	Laborer	pneumonia
320	NORRIS Mary C	1		De	Apr		pneumonia
367	BIDDLE Tobias R	75	m		Feb	Farmer	paralysis
373	FITZHUGH Maria	70B	w		Jan		paralysis
373	AYERS Jonathan	81	m		May	Forgeman	paralysis
373	MAHAN Elizabeth	75	w		Jun		paralysis
378	WORDELL Emma	2			Nov		croup
395	BROOKS John	76			May	Gunsmith	inflamation bladder
404	FLOUNDERS Sarah	11			Oct		diptheria
404	FLOUNDERS Edward	1			Nov		diptheria

TOWN of ELKTON - CECIL COUNTY 1870

61	PURNELL Enoch M	28		Mch	Clerk drygood	phthsis pulmonary
75	DAVIS Isabella	3/12		Apr		mesenterica
80	BUTLER Joseph Loper	20		Aug	Domestic	phthsis pulmonary
78	MACKEY Annie M	10		Aug		typhoid fever
112	MYERS M A	f2/12		Aug		cholera infantum
172	DONOVAN no name	f1/12B		Feb		marasmus
160	WILSON Edward	54	w	Sep	Fisherman	pneumonia
162	BROWN Mary Ella	2/12B		Feb		congestion lungs
	EVANS Abraham	78B	m	Feb	Laborer	carbuncle
203	ROBINSON Mary V	22		Aug		lung disease
210	CROSBY Fatima	70	w	Jun		paralysis
233	MAHAN Joseph L	34	m	Aug	Postmaster	chronic diarrhea
224	JONES Clinton	1		Jan		croup
225	PERKINS A Matlack	5/12		Jun		cholera infantum
231	SCOTT Lula May	7/12		Apr		pneumonia
242	DAVIS _____	f60B		Apr	Washwoman	uterine disease
291	HAMMON James	59B	m	Jan	Laborer	heart disease
310	HAYES William S	1/12B		Dec		
330	PIERSON William D	14/30		Jun 1st		marasmus
372	HEMPHIL Joseph	52	m	Jan		delerium

5	ANDERSON Robert J	2		p fo	Feb		scrofula
10	STRAHORN Martha Ann	60	m	Pa	Feb	Keeping house	aneurism
79	STUARD Nellie	5		Pa	Mch		scarlet fever
135	SCOTT Elvira	62	w	De	Feb	Keeping house	aneurism
161	ALEXANDER George W	4		De	Sep		chronic dysentary
185	WILLIS Sarah C	35	m		Mch	Keeping house	consumption
194	WORK Ettie A	2			Aug		scarlet fever
3	EVANS Leslie Elmer	2/12			Feb		scrofula
207	SAXTON Edward F	1/12			Apr		aneurism
235	GALLAHER Ann Jane	55	m		Apr	Keeping house	disease of heart
255	CALEB James Alfred	33	m	De	Apr	Farmer	consumption
280	LOVE May	3/12			Aug		dysentary
289	VINSINGER Ruth A	31		Pa	May	House keeper	inflamation bowels
310	REEDER Joseph Henry	4			Jan		disease of brain
319	JANNEY Margaret	72	m		Sep	Keeping house	consumption
329	DOWD Laura	1/12			Mch		epilepsy
331	McCAULEY Anna	68	m	Pa	May	Keeping house	typhoid fever
358	BROWN Kate McVey	1B			Mch		consumption
360	EWING John	76	m	Ir	Oct	Farmer	cancer stomach
379	WOOLENS Jesse	79	m	Pa	Jan	Farmer	apoplexy
380	ANDERSON William F	1		Pa	Sep		consumption
394	HOLTON Margaret C	4		Pa	Feb		scrofula
3	EVANS Gassaway	3			Apr		typhoid fever

DISTRICT #5 - CECIL COUNTY 1870

33	LYNCH Margaret Jane	3			Mch		fall
60	McBEY James	80	w		Mch	Farmer	pneumonia
71	ALEXANDER Margaret	48	m		Mch	Keeping house	change of life
107	CURRY Henry H	18			Mch	Laborer	consumption
114	MURRY James	76	m	En	May	Farmer	dyspepsia
127	PARMER Mary R	27	m		Jun	Keeping house	consumption
154	JOHNSON Andrew	30B	m		Feb	Farm hand	measles
169	STEVENSON Richard	70B	m		Apr	Farm hand	dropsy
175	JOHNSON Sarah	4B			Jun		burnt to death
184	CRESWELL Amos	35	w		Jun	Farmer	consumption
198	McKINNEY John A	21			Feb	Farmer	disease of brain
211	HAMMOND Vincent	64	m	En	Mch	Farmer	rheumatism
218	COOK Charles	7/12			Feb		pneumonia
230	GORDON Dorcas	28B	m		Mch	Keeping house	pneumonia
238	KNOX Mary	55	m	De	Aug		stroke
245	GURDY John	35	m	Pa	Jun	Farmer	killed on railroad
255	THOMAS John	2			Jul		diarrhea
290	McCALLOUGH Elizabeth	39	m		Apr	Keeping house	consumption
314	DEAN Elizabeth	4			Jul		scarlet fever
342	TUCKER Samuel	29	m		Sep	Carpenter	cut with an ax
365	CLEMONS Nancy	72	m		Mch	House keeper	consumption

#	Name	Age			Month	Occupation	Cause
373	CRAMER William	23	w		Jan	Miller	consumption
430	CRAWFORD James	69	w	Ir	Mch	Woolen manufac	diarrhea
440	ATKINSON Francis	63	w		Apr	Farmer	consumption
449	MORRIS Theophilus	3B			Mch		consumption
449	MORRIS Anna	6/12B			Nov		lung disease
452	BENJAMIN George E	1			Sep		liver disease
453	BURNS Clara E	4			Oct		croup
466	MORRELL Lewis N	35	m	Pa	May	Wheelwright	consumption
474	CUNNINGHAM Margaret	57	m		Nov	Keeping house	erysipelas
481	SEARS Charlotte	4B			Apr		inflammation bowels
489	HEATH John	75	m		Jan	Farmer	pneumonia
508	BROWN Abraham	50B	m		Dec	Farm hand	consumption
508	BROWN George	4B			May		pneumonia

BOROUGHS of N.E. & CHARLESTOWN - CECIL COUNTY

#	Name	Age			Month	Occupation	Cause
10	WILSON Andrew	73	m		Feb	Sea Captain	disease in bowels
16	MURPHY Edward	1			Jul		inflammation brain
25	DAVIS Rachel	41	m		Apr	Keeping house	childbirth
32	LARDNER Frances	3			Jun		heart disease
37	BENJAMIN Fanny A	13			Mch		burnt

BOROUGH of CHARLESTOWN CECIL COUNTY

#	Name	Age			Month	Occupation	Cause
11	BENNETT William H	4			Aug		dysentary
14	SMITH Martha	3/12			Mch		consumption
20	COOLING Orman	6/12			Mch		debility
35	RICHARDSON Charles	5			Aug		dysentary

DISTRICT #6 - CECIL COUNTY 1870

#	Name	Age			Month	Occupation	Cause
314	SMITH Ida	2			Aug		consumption
314	SMITH Margaret	5/12			Aug		whooping cough
3	NESBITT Eleanor	5			Apr		consumption
3	NESBITT Clara	67	m		May	Keeping House	consumption
72	MORRISON Robert	78	w		Feb	Farmer	pneumonia
154	SHELLY Elizabeth	66	m		Feb	Keeping house	apoplexy
157	SUTER Rachel E	5			May		bilious fever
167	KIRK William	75	w		Dec	Millwright	dropsy
174	TYSON Nathan	2			Sep		lung disease
183	PHILLIPS Elizabeth	2			Apr		catarrh of breast
182	HART John	67	w	Ir	Jun	Laborer	inflammation bowels
193	BROWN Robert	78B	m		Feb	Laborer	inflammation liver
210	BRUMFIELD Amelia	79	m		May	Keeping house	consumption
250	BRICKLEY Andrew	74	m		May	Farmer	apoplexy
258	EAGAN Marian E	62	w	NY	Jun	Keeping house	consumption
259	PHILLIPS Elvira	1			Apr		pneumonia
272	McDOUGLE Mary	60	m	Ir	Mch	Keeping house	consumption
274	SMITH William	76	m	Ir	Jun		consumption
295	BONSAL Naomi	57	m	Pa	Aug	Keeping house	paralysis
301	TERRY Mary K	8/12			May		consumption

302	McCULLOUGH Lucy	61	w		Feb	House keeper	paralysis
393	MOORE Carrie	7			Feb		typhoid fever
437	MAGNAN Emily	59	m		May	House keeper	typhoid fever

BOROUGH of RISING SUN

12	KIMBLE Cora	3			May		pyemia
15	KIRK Timmie	3/12			Jul		diarrhea
49	KIRK Esther	3/12			Jul		cholera infantum

PORT DEPOSIT - CECIL COUNTY

8	PEOPLES George	11/12		p/fb	Jan		measles
9	BURK Rebecca	40	m	Ir	Apr	Keeping house	puerperal fever
69	CATHERS Rebecca	24			Jan	Milliner	consumption
123	LAWRENCE George	1			Jan		measles
124	LAWRENCE Isaiah	53	m		Dec	Stone Cutter	heart disease
157	DAVIS Jane	72	w		May		paralysis
161	COOK Elizabeth	5/12			Apr		cholera infantum
178	MORRISON Elizabeth	45	m	De	Jun	Keeping house	pneumonia
223	THOMAS Mary	25B	m		Apr	Keeping house	pneumonia
224	SULIVAN John	1		p/fb	Sep		whooping cough
235	McCLANAHAN Ann	7			May		heart disease
238	BUCK Annie	1		f/fb	Dec		convulsions
240	NOTLY Elizabeth	3/12			Aug		convulsions
273	HARRIMAN Charles	2/12		Pa	Jul		cholera infantum

DISTRICT #8 - CECIL COUNTY 1870

52	KERNS Sarah J	28	m	Pa	Jul	Keeping house	child bed
128	TILLMAN Catharine	2B			May		infection lungs
184	GILLESPIE William	55	m		Mch	Farmer	brain disease
221	FULTON John	78	w	Pa	Jun	Carpenter	paralysis
248	McKINEY John	77	w	Pa	May	Farmer	old age

DISTRICT #9 - CECIL COUNTY 1870

8	BROWN Huldah	78	w		May	House keeper	paralysis
10	ALGARD Josephine E	3			Nov		scarlet fever
12	MOORE Hannah	76	w	Pa	Jan	House keeper	consumption
42	KIRK Emma	17			Mch		pneumonia
50	HARVEY Margaret	1		p/fb	May		convulsions
54	McVEY Rachel	70	m		Dec	House keeper	disease of abdomen
54	McVEY James	82	w		Mch	Farmer	consumption
64	CROUSE Susan Ann	63	m		Jan	Keeping house	paralysis
81	ROGERS William	60	w		Feb		scrofula
103	BROWN Kirk	57	m	Pa	Jul	Laborer	consumption
116	IRWIN Harriet	21			Aug		typhoid fever
134	BENNIKER Mary	20	m	f/fb	Aug	Keeping house	brain fever
179	KIRK Margaret L	37	m		Apr	Keeping house	consumption
229	MAHANNEY bigail	76	m		May	House keeper	diabetes
236	REEDER William	82	m	Pa	Jan	Farmer	pneumonia

257	CHANDLER Ellis G	5B	m		Jan	Merchant	aneurism
257	CHANDLER Phebe A	22	m	Pa	Nov	Keeping house	aneurism
293	MURRAY Eugenia	2/12			Jul		scarlet fever
65	PAXSON Luanna	10			Feb		scarlet fever

DISTRICT #7 - CECIL COUNTY 1870

1	KNIGHT John	70	w	Pa	Jan	Quarry laborer	killed by RR car
3	DUNKARD Mary	1/12			Jan		unknown
5	PHILIPS Julia	5/12			Jan		cholera infantum
7	GLASS Mary	1/12			Nov		cholera infantum
57	BENWELL William	52	m	Pa	Jul	Farmer	dropsy
62	DUKEHART Mary	8/12			Aug		consumption
88	BOYD Jane	4/12			Dec		dysentary
129	McMARTIN Robert	28	m		May	Carpenter	consumption
165	FRANKLIN Joseph	14B			Feb	Laborer	consumption
185	HAINES Henry	26	m		Jul	Cabinet maker	consumption
237	HARRIS Acey	69	m		Aug	Keeping house	pneumonia
242	BOYD Francis	78	m		May	Farmer	heart disease
249	THOMPSON Henry	1/12			Jan		unknown
259	MITCHELL Maria	16B			Aug	works out	consumption
261	ADDISON George	42B	m		Feb	Farm worker	hemorrhagic gums
269	TAYLOR Miflin	1B			Mch		convulsions
293	JACKSON Amelia	19			Dec		measles
306	LINTON Sarah	35	m		Sep	Keeping house	consumption
307	BULLIN Robert	14			Sep		lung disease
339	GREGG Jonathan	90	m	Sct	May	Laborer	old age
340	WILSON Nicolis	42			Feb	Laborer	typhoid fever
341	RONEY Robert	5/12			Jan		croup
361	RUSSELL Elizabeth	87	w	Ir	Feb		dropsy
367	GIBSON George	10B			Feb		disease heart
375	STUMP Elizabeth	25	w		Jun		consumption
277	ALEXANDRIA Mary	57	m	Va	Sep	Keeping house	typhoid fever
277	ALEXANDRIA Mary	63			Mch		pneumonia
369	PHYSIC Edward	81	m		Feb		old age
369	PHYSIC Mary	60	m		Mch	Keeping house	pleurisy

No.	Name	Age			Month	Occupation	Cause
5	HOWETH Charlotte	11/12			Mch		croup
12	MURPHY Eliza	60	m		Feb		consumption
13	COLLISON Mary	5/12			Aug		congestion-chill
22	MURPHY Elizabeth	2			Feb		pneumonia
31	BELL Cyrus	57	m		Jun	Farmer	typhoid
32	CEPHAS Hardy	23B	m		Aug	Sailor	drowned
	CEPHAS Elsey	2B			Feb		measles
54	BLADES Benjamin	46	m		Dec		murdered
59	TULL Milla R	4			Nov		pneumonia
96	WALLACE Thomas	63	w	De	Nov	Miller	cancer
100	STOKES George	25	m		Feb	Sailor	consumption
112	COOPER William	57	m	De	Aug	Laborer	inflammation bowels
113	JOHNSON Alice	2B			Sep		swelling
114	CORNISH Hannah	52B	m		May	Keeping house	abcess in side
156	COLLINS Peter	2/12B			Feb		croup
157	STILES Mary	50	m	De	Aug	Keeping house	consumption
168	LOWE William	8/12			Jul		typhoid
175	HOBBS Charles E	8/12			May		diarrhea
176	WAINWRIGHT Margaret	45		De	Mch		consumption
212	JOHNS May	35B	m		Jun		consumption
-	JOHNS Manuel	23B	m		Dec	Soldier	consumption
229	ADAMS Minos	73	w		Dec	Farmer	old age
240	MARINE Amanda	4			Jul		diarrhea
263	WHEATLEY Minos	2/12			Jul		croup
269	DAVIS Grace	70	w		Dec	Farmer	consumption
-	DAVIS Amelia A	60	w		Aug	Keeping house	comsumption
270	REED Ezekiel	14			Oct		typhoid

DISTRICT #2 - DORCHESTER COUNTY 1870

No.	Name	Age			Month	Occupation	Cause
	Mary	4B			Jul		inflammation bowel
17	NESBITT Sallie M	2/12			Jul		unknown
19	REED Harriet E	3/12			Aug		inflammation brain
30	WILLOUGHBY Annie	4/12			Apr		whooping cough
33	JOSHUA Johnson	2B			Feb		unknown
56	LEE Mary	64B	w		Jun		consumption
	ROSS Samuel	5/12B			Jul		pneumonia
72	ALLEN Henry	73B	m		Nov	Laborer	consumption
112	CORNISH Mary	4/12B			Jul		unknown
132	PAGE William	30	m		Oct	Farmer	pneumonia
139	CHARLES William M	4/12			Jul		whooping cough
165	BAKER John	58	m		May	Farmer	pneumonia
200	DAVIS Elizabeth	50	w		Feb	Keeping house	paralysis
205	PARKER Mary E	13B			May		pneumonia
211	WRIGHT Lucreta	2/12			Oct		unknown
222	CONWAY Thomas	1B			Dec		unknown
234	BANKS John	3/12B			Oct		unknown
237	McGRATH Mary	2			Jul		dysentary

251	DAVIS Samuel P	33	m	De	May	Farmer	spotted fever
255	WILOUGHBY Ann	67	w		May	Keeping house	consumption
261	RIDEOUT Winfield	2B			Jul		diarrhea
261	RIDEOUT James	1B			Oct		diarrhea
268	NICOLS John	23B			Feb	Laborer	consumption
271	KENNY William	10/12			Oct		unknown
272	MOONEY William	68	m		Feb		pneumonia
282	HOLLOW Joanna	13B			Sep		pneumonia
282	HOLLOW Edward	7B			Oct		pneumonia
285	YOUNG Washington	2/12B			Aug		diarrhea
285	YOUNG James	3/12B			Sep		unknown
286	WATERS John	1B			Dec		diarrhea
321	WILLOUGHBY Job	45	m		Mch	Farmer	pneumonia
330	ABDELL Sallie	2			Jan		inflammation brain
335	MOORE Anna	73	w		May		consumption
356	SAXTON Linda	7			Feb		pneumonia
356	SAXTON Grace	4			Feb		pneumonia
357	_____ Anna	f1			Oct		cholera infantum
362	WILSON Elizabeth	30	m	Va	Nov	Keeping house	pneumonia
367	_____ _____	m1/12			Mch		unknown
3--	_____ _____	f1			Oct		cholera infantum
3--	_____ _____	m63	m		Jul		inflammation bowels
4-2	_____ Mary	36B	w		Jun69		consumption

DISTRICT #3 - DORCHESTER COUNTY 1870

-	LYONS Sarah A	59	w		Apr	Keeping house	apoplexy
31	JOHNSON William	2			Aug		cholera infantum
32	ANDERSON Amanda	43	m		Jan	Keeping house	inflammation stomach
35	DIVINE Emily	80B	w	f/fb	Mch		pneumonia
44	WEBB Theodore	23			Aug	Clerk	consumption
45	SMITHERS Edward S	18			Oct	Taught School	lock jaw
51	ROBINSON Robert	14B			Jan	Farm worker	bronchitis
66	HENRY Harriet	3/12M			Feb		unknown
66	HENRY Lulia	3/12M			Feb		unknown
89	LORD George	5			Sep		unknown
93	McALLISTER William	4			Oct		congestive chill
93	McALLISTER Minos	1			Mch		croup
119	MURPHY Samuel	2/12			Mch		croup
125	TILLMAN Ann	6/12B			Nov		unknown
144	FLEMING Ella	3			Oct		pneumonia
159	HARPER Milda	27	m		Jul	Keeping house	typhoid fever
159	no name	1/12			Jul		unknown
173	RAWLEIGH Rachel	43	m		Mch	Keeping house	fever
183	CEPHUS Josephine	3/12B			Dec		unknown
202	COLEMAN Leah	4/12B			May		whooping cough
	HOLLIS Delia	16B			Oct		consumption
212	DENWOOD Henry	50B			Nov	Farmer	found dead in woods
224	BAILY Peter	110B	w		Aug		old age
236	WILEY Mary	60	m		Jun		measles
242	WILLEY Solomon	2/12			Mch		unknown
245	DEAN Mary	100			Mch		pneumonia

7	DIES Margaret	1/12		Mch		unknown
17	ADAMS Frances	3/12		May		unknown
22	WINGATE Joseph	2		Jul		dropsey
82	TODD Elisha	33	m	May	Oysterman	typhoid fever
133	MOORE Risdon S	23	m	Oct	Oysterman	brain fever
142	WILLY Columbia	7		Sep		diptheria
151	TODD Elizabeth	46	m	Dec	Keeping house	typhoid fever
151	TODD Lorenzo	1/12		Feb		unknown
154	TODD Samuel	1		Jul		scalded
159	not named	1/12		Nov		unknown
3	EDGER William H	33	m	Aug	Farmer	unknown
5	FOXWELL Wilda A	19	m	Nov	Keeping house	brain fever
5	FOXWELL Mary J	5/12		Jan		pneumonia
39	WROTEN Cordelia	11		Dec		typhoid fever
46	PRITCHETT Samuel	1B		Jun		unknown
50	GRIFFIN Hester	60B	w	Mch	Keeping house	pneumonia
57	KIRWIN Edward	1		Mch		croup
59	WROTEN Robert R	1		Dec		diptheria
109	not named	1/12		Feb		unknown
111	MOORE Isaac	55	m	Mch	Farmer	pneumonia
116	JONES Levin P	23		Jun	Oysterman	dysentary
119	BRAWARD Julia Ann	60	w	Sep		unknown
120	SHENTON Anna	64	w	Aug	Keeping house	dysentary
126	STEWART Malinda	1		Sep		unknown
131	SLACUM Mary	16		Sep		typhoid fever
131	SLACUM Louisa	6		Dec		typhoid fever
135	SHORTER Cain	64	m	Aug	Farm worker	heart disease
140	MASON Nancy	44	w	May		erysipelas
189	not named	1/12		Mch		unknown
202	TREXLER Elizabeth	34	m	Sep	Keeping house	apoplexy
202	TREXLER Sarah F	5/12		Mch		unknown
206	ROBINSON Lucinda	87	w	Mch	Keeping house	old age
205	INSLEY George	60		Mch	Farmer	unknown
220	TYLER Oliver P	20		Feb	Farmer	pneumonia
19	MOORE Thomas S	41	m	Aug	Farmer	unknown

DISTRICT #5,#6,#4 - DORCHESTER COUNTY 1870

152	ANDERSON Emily	11		Nov		croup
162	ROSS Thomas	14B		Sep		dropsey
163	KIRWIN Mary	59	m	Sep	Keeping house	pneumonia
168	WALLACE Margaret	21		Oct		typhoid fever
240	KEENE James	18B		Oct	Farm laborer	scarlet fever
240	KEENE Susann	8B		Aug		scarlet fever
244	SHENTON Alice	3/12		Dec		unknown
245	KEENE Minty	35B		Jan		consumption
256	TODD Nancy	50	m	Mch		consumption
256	DUNNOCK Oliver W	11		Dec		typhoid fever
255	BENNETT Mary	6B		Mch		burnt to death
202	PINDER Charles	41B	m	May	Farmer	heart disease
205	CHESTER John R	1/12B		Apr		unknown
206	SCHOFIELD Peter	2B		Aug		dysentary

192	WARD William	76	w		Aug	Miller	fever-inflam leg
194	ROBINSON Edwin	2			Jul		dysentary
195	REAGAN Sarah	28	m		Mch	Keeping house	unknown
2	REDDITT James	30	m	Sct	Dec	Farmer	diptheria
4	HILL Jennie	3			Sep		measles
45	BANE Luther	70	m		Feb	Farmer	consumption
91	KEENE Arianna	30B			Mch		consumption

DISTRICT #8, #7 - DORCHESTER COUNTY 1870

104	ROBINS Sarah C	3			Jul		dysentary
113	RHEA William	76	m	Sct	Jul	School teacher	old age
113	RHEA Mary	4		p/fb	Jul		dysentary
113	THOMAS Robert C	18			Dec		typhoid fever
129	THOMAS John B	7			Aug		dysentary
144	THOMAS Robert	14			Dec		typhoidfever
149	HUBBARD Dora	9			Sep		typhoid fever
152	FLETCHER Nancy	11/12B			Apr		pneumonia
158	NORTH Harriet	77	m		Feb	Keeping house	old age
172	SEWARD Levin	14			Apr		pneumonia
185	NORTH Alice K	3			Sep		diptheria
9	JONES Mary	3/12B			May		whooping cough
9	JONES Martha	3/12B			May		consumption
8	BYUS Mary	12B			Apr		consumption
17	THOMAS Edward	65	m		Jul	Farmer	unknown
17	THOMAS Frances	17			Jun		pneumonia
17	LINTHICUM Frances	85	w		May		old age
18	BRAWARD Sallie	5/12			Apr		unknown
19	MARSHALL John	6/12			Aug		cholera infantum
25	MOORE John T	38	m		Sep	Farmer	consumption
33	BOWDIN Severn	30		Va	Mch	Sailor	exposure
40	MOBRAY Cuthbert	55	w		Mch	Carpenter	pneumonia
42	TODD Wilda	7/12			Jul		cholera infantum
91	LOWE Clara	26	m		Oct	Keeping house	consumption
91	LOWE Anna M	7/12			Mch		consumption
106	SULLIVAN William	62			Apr		debility
125	RUDENSTEIN John	45	m		Dec	Surgeon USN	pneumonia
145	BRYAN James	1			Oct		consumption
148	COOK William	2			May		unknowni
162	CORNISH Mary L	9B			Dec		pneumonia
162	CORNISH Josiah	6B			Mch		consumption
175	BURTON Mary	60B	m		Jun	Dom servant	unknown
197	WINGATE Margaret	52	w		Jan	Keeping house	disease of uterus
217	WOOLFORD Robert H	1B			Aug		inflammation bowels
222	CAMPER Mary E	1/12			Apr		inflammation bowels

DISTRICT #7 - DORCHESTER COUNTY 1870

239	SMITH Annie	5B			Apr		unknown
253	LEE John	56B	m		Jun	Drayman	consumption
254	MOORE Harriet	14B			Jul		consumption

36	TRAVERS Moses	30B	Jul	Sailor	typhoid fever
37	PARKS Robert	14	Oct		drowned
39	WALSH Thomas	3	Nov		worms
56	CREIGHTON Madira	3	Aug		unknown
60	TYLER mary	13	Aug		dysentary
63	ADAMS Robert R	24	Feb	Sailor	drowned
67	PRITCHETT John H	2	Apr		burnt to death
83	CREIGHTON Matthew	10	Oct		dysentary
83	PARKER Mary	78	Feb		pneumonia
102	BARNES Elizabeth	22B m	Jun		child birth
117	MEEKINS Caroline	60 m	Oct		unknown
28	SPICER Travers	70 m	Feb	Farmer	pneumonia
30	WILLEY Sophia	60 m	Aug		consumption
31	DAVIS Isaac H	69 m	Jun	Ship carpenter	pneumonia
31	SANDERS Sarah	72 m	Jul		unknown
45	HOOPER Catherine	27B m	Aug	Keeping house	consumption
62	PALMER Elizabeth	55	Jun	Keeping house	cancer
82	TOLLY John T	28 m	Jan	Farmer	consumption
104	KIRE Joseph	41B m	Jan	Farm laborer	pneumonia
135	DUNNOCK Emily	1B	Jan		unknown
151	WOOLFORD Julia Ann	1/12	Jan		unknown

DISTRICT #4,#9,#8 -- DORCHESTER COUNTY 1870

168	TRAVERS Perry	32 m	Feb	Farm laborer	pneumonia
171	HARRIS Samuel	71B m	Jul	Farmer	old age
172	DUNNOCK Ernest	4	Sep		unknown
172	DUNNOCK Samuel	7	Mch		unknown
180	LINTHICUM Amelia	2B	Apr		unknown
194	SANDERS Annie	25 m	Dec	Keeping house	pneumonia
199	SMITH Frances	1	Aug		diarrhea
207	OTHER John W	2B	May		whooping cough
206	BROWN Melvina	12B	Jun		measles
232	MILLS Roseann	31 m	Aug	Milliner	inflammation bowels
242	HARRINGTON Elizabeth	50 m	Aug	Keeping house	unknown
244	HARRINGTON Carlton	8/12	Nov		unknown
254	CROMWELL Alice	65B m	Jul		erysipelas
264	FARQUARHARSON John	6/12B	Oct		unknown
291	MACER James H	3/12	Sep		unknown
2	not named	1/12	Nov		unknown
18	WELLS John E	2	Apr		throat disease
18	WELLS John E	2	Apr		throat disease
105	KEENE John W	24	Feb		pneumonia
50	HICKS Isabelle	2B	Jun		consumption
50	CHESTER John W	6/12B	Jun		scrofula
71	CAMPER Ann	2B	Jun		unknown
80	BOWLEY Lina	62B	Apr	Dom servant	consumption
106	CAMPER Elizabeth	17B m	Mch		child birth
141	YOUNG Mary	30B	Feb		consumption
148	MOWBRAY Sallie	70	Mch		apoplexy
180	MILES Harriet	71B	Jul		old age
189	CORNISH George	9B	Jul		inflammation bowels
190	CAMPER Elijah	20B	Jan	Farm laborer	consumption

255	LANE Luella	2B	Dec		consumption
262	HUMAN Samuel	2/12B	Dec		croup
263	not named	1/12B	Mch		croup
269	FORD Margaret	1B	May		croup
275	PRITCHETT Rebecca	22B	Dec		scrofula
277	YOUNG Susan	39B m	Dec	Keeping house	dropsey
279	BALL Jane	40B m	May	Keeping house	intermittant fever
292	EWING Amelia	36B m	Sep	Keeping house	dropsey
302	WRIGHTSON Mary	60 w	Feb		consumption
6	HUMAN Samuel	6/12B	Oct		consumption
10	NEAL Leah	70B w	Oct	Dom servant	old age
31	TUBMAN Annie	11B	Dec		explosion of coaloil
66	JENKINS Lucy	85B w	May		dropsey
96	THOMAS Samuel	1/12	Jul		unknown
96	THOMAS Mary E	1/12	Jul		unknown
148	WROTEN Emma	11	May		dyptheria
148	WROTEN Clara V	8	May		dyptheria
163	HOLLIDAY John E	4/12B	Sep		cholera infantum
212	ECCLESTON Susan	61 w	Jul		heart disease
234	FARRARA Caroline	55B	Mch		unknown
233	PARSON Milton	16	Mch		pneumonia
255	SHUMAN Charles	21	Apr		drowned
268	WRIGHT Noble	73 m	Nov	Farmer	pneumonia
268	WRIGHT Sallie	60 w	Nov	Keeping house	pneumonia

DISTRICT #11 - DORCHESTER COUNTY 1870

10	ROBINSON Mary	49B m	Mch	Keeping house	intermittant fever
46	FISHER louisa	1	Apr		whooping cough
55	HORSEMAN	1	Sep		unknown
87	HACHET Eliza	10B	Feb		pneumonia
87	JACKSON Stephen	69B	Jan		typhoid
95	not named	1/12B	Dec		croup
119	LORD Margaret	23 m	Oct		consumption
120	WILSON May	1B	Apr		unknown
138	KIAH Uriah	37B m	Aug		unknown
147	YOUNG Amy	43B m	Oct		consumption
149	KEEN Thomas	43B w	Oct	Pauper	A
	ADKINSON Thomas	85B m	Jul	"	L
	JOHNSON Ann	70 w	Aug	"	M
	BRYAN Ann	60B m	Jun 69	"	S
	HARMON Fina	40B m	Mch	"	
	BLAKE Moses	45B	Feb	Pauper	H
	YOUNG James	42B w	Mch	"	O
	GAINES James	55B	Apr	"	U
	ELLIS Henry	30B	May	Pauper	S
152	CHASE Noah	4B	Jul		E
161	MOLOCH Noah	24B	Mch		consumption
162	____ John	2/12B	Jan		croup
162	CEPHAS William	11/12B	Feb		unknown
173	MEREDITH Pritchet	60 w	Dec	Farmer	typhoid fever

14	MOORE Mary	68	w		Mch	Keeping house	pneumonia
38	DICKERSON Lydia	1B			Oct		croup
40	CEPHAS Charles	11/12B			Nov		pneumonia
41	BUNINGTON John	25B			Feb	Late soldier	consumption
41	LOGAN William C	21			Dec		consumption
46	KILLMON Elizabeth F	1M			Mch		burnt to death
58	BLACKSHIRE Margaret	50	m	Pa	Mch	Keeping house	consumption
92	STACK James	89	w		Mch	Ret Farmer	dropsey on chest
102	WRIGHT Constant	35	m		Jun69	Farmer	consumption
124	DAVIS Bernie	1			Feb		whooping cough
136	BRYAN William H	4			Jun69		typhoid
161	CORKRAN Charles	11			Dec		congestive chill
163	BOWDLE Mary	11			Jan		typhoid
164	ROWINGS Mary	1			Aug		typhoid
170	DAWSON Levan	60	m		Jun69	Farmer	pneumonia
226	ANDREW Charles	57	w		Aug	Sailor	consumption

27	YOUNG Josephine	2B		Feb	croup
28	STANLY Sarah	88B	w	Jan	unknown
39	YOUNG Joseph	71B	w	Apr	rheumatism
49	HANDY Purnel	62B		Sep	apoplexy
72	HEATH H ___	51B	m	Dec	consumption
76	HOLLAND Henry	76B	m	May	typhoid fever
96	HUGHES Mary	8B		Jun 69	pneumonia
98	CORNISH Aaron	45B	m	Feb	heart disease
115	GRIFFIN Daniel	65B		Dec	typhoid fever
115	CORNISH Aaron	60B	m	Apr	unknown fever
136	STANDLY Dorithy	25B	m	May	consumption
143	MEREDITH Pritchet	2/12		May	inflammation bowels
144	TRAVERS John	51B	m	Aug	bowel disease

	BRADLEY M Robert	1/12		Oct		brain fever
12	___ ___	2		Aug		brain fever
26	___ Perry	30B		Apr	Farm hand	pneumonia
35	BALL H___	m77	De	Jun		old age
57	PRICE ___	9/12		May		unknown
61	_____ Mary	63 w	De	Aug		
72	DUKES Charles	20		Feb	Farm laborer	
73	BENSON	-/12M		Dec		
	BENSON Fanny	0/12M		May		
74	MARTIN Lewis	6/12		Sep		cholera infantum
94	___ ___	1/12B		May		
95	BENSON Ida	2/12B		May		
96	FISHER John	1/12B		Jul		
110	DAVIS ___	m30B m		Apr		
114	DAVIS John	22B		Mch		
115	BUTLER Emily	15B		May		typhoid fever
	BUTLER Maria	9B		May		typhoid fever
	BUTLER E ___	m6B		May		scrofula
	BUTLER Dan	11B		Sep		typhoid fever
133	____ Sarah	36 m		Aug		typhoid fever
143	___ John	6/12		Feb		congestive chill
144	KNIGHT Isaac	30 m		Sep	Blacksmith	hernia
144	___ W___	m2		May		epilepsy
151	___	f22 m		Jun		
151	___ A Maria	1		Jun		
1-7	BLAKE Ann	63M w		May		
2-3	C_ James	82 w		Oct	Carpenter	paralysis
2-6	C_____ Mary	70 m		Nov		old age
251	SPARKS ___	m7/12		Jun		unknown
	SPARKS _____	17		Feb		
275	ADKINSON Laura	1		Nov		croup
---	SUTTON Harriet	6/12B		Dec		croup
281	BANKS ____	m30		Mch	Farm laborer	pneumonia
293	R___ Laurance	37 m		Aug		inflammation brain
314	BURGESS Thomas	71 m		Feb	Farmer	pneumonia
330	_____ _____	21		Oct		
	_____ _____	2/12B		Sep		
3--	_____ Laura V	1/12B		Aug		
3-6	JOHNSON Henry	25B m		Jun	Farm laborer	
3-7	_____ Alexander	32B		Jun		

| 261 | TEAT Laura | 1/12 | | May | | unknown |
| 283 | MORTON James | 45B w | | Feb | | consumption |

Sassafras

15	ROBERTS John T	25	De	Feb	Merchant	scrofula
34	JOHNS Sarah	4/12B		Feb		fever
48	WACKETT James	50B m		Apr	Laborer	consumption

Galena

13	PRICE Joanna	5B		May		cholera infantum
19	CAMP James	1		May		cholera infantum
44	SUTTON Orlando	53 m		Oct	Cartwright	consumption

First Election District

323	CAULK Jacob	80 w	De	Feb	Farmer	cancer
345	CLAYTON Jacob	86 w	De	Mch	Farmer	old age
356	McNATT William	4		Oct		cholera infantum
357	NEWTON George H	9/12		May		cholera infantum
368	ANDERSON James	2/12B		May		unknown
384	McKENNY Benjamin	5B		May		billious fever
402	SALISBURY Thomas	1/12B		Jun		colic
407	BRICE William N	31 m		Jul	Merchant	typhoid fever
408	HEMPHREY Julia	21 m		Jun		childbirth
409	DESHANE Ann R	55 m		Jan		disease of womb
420	PEEKER Rachel	5B		May		consumption
420	PEEKER Vermadilla	1/12B		May		mortification naval
443	NANCE Isaac	67	NJ	Dec	Ret Sailor	consumption
443	MARTEN Mary	100B w		Nov		dropsy
482	CAULK Alfred	33B w		Apr	Laborer	consumption
488	CAULK John Eddy	8/12B		Oct		unknown
499	WILMER Renetta S	3B		May		liver affection
501	SCOTT Hester A	1B		May		dysentary
510	RASIN Ann E	54 m		Mch		cancer
525	MILLER Lee	2		Apr		measles

Millington

8	MANN Joseph	64 m		Apr	Miller	consumption
23	NUMBERS Margaret W	2		Nov		unknown
24	McCAULEY Ann	35 m	Ir	Jul	House keeper	breast cancer
50	ANDERSON Sity Howard	3/12		Dec		
55	WILMORE Harriet	36B w		Mch		childbirth
57	BECK Henrietta	2B		Mch		pneumonia
43	THOMAS Sarah E	28		Mch		paralysis

First Election District

7	Mayson Ida	1/12B		Feb		lung disease
13	RILEY John E	25B		Jun	Laborer	consumption
47	SMITH Elizabeth	4		Nov		croup
53	ROCHESTER Howard	2B		Apr		fever
61	MARKEY Susan A	22B		Jul	House Keeper	consumption
74	DAVIS Jacob	2		Dec		scarlet fever
73	EMTRAY William	25?	Pa	Jun		billious fever
106	WILSON Susan	30		Dec		consumption
106	THOMPSON Ellen	2B		Feb		scrofula
111	McGUIRE George	39 m		Sep	Laborer	dropsy
116	BROWN Sarah M	46		Sep		pleurisy

123 KNOX Mary A	18		Jul			childbirth
123 KNOX Charles	2		Jul			diarrhea
123 WHITTINGTON William T	8/12		Jul			fits from teething
143 PORTER John S	50 m		Mch	Farmer		asthma
145 HOLDEN John T	29		Mch	Farmer		typhoid
148 MOFFETT Enoch E	1/12		Mch			pneumonia
166 SMITH John F	55 m	De	Jan	Farmer		consumption
188 CROSSLEY Mary A	35 m	De	Feb			consumption

Chesterville

16 GARRETT William	12		May			remittant fever

First Election District

190 SMITH Samuel	27		Sep	Laborer		suicide/strychnine
191 HODGSON Jonathan	8/12		Feb			inflammation brain
217 MANDEN John	19B		May	Laborer		billious fever
219 WIGGENS Anna	52 w		Jun			consumption
219 WIGGENS infant	5/12		Oct			unknown
248 BARN Clinton	30		Nov	Laborer		pneumonia
257 CLARK Rachel C	7/12		Feb			scrofula
257 THOMAS Charles	7/12		May			spinal deffect

? DISTRICT #2 - KENT COUNTY 1870

WRIGHT Mille	40B		Nov		dropsy
SAMPSON Annie	21B		Sep		consumption
WRIGHT Joseph	7B		Jul		unknown
WRIGHT Hannah	17B		Feb		consumption
WILSON Henry	1B		---		unknown
BOSEE John	72		Sep	Farmer	chronic dysentary
SPARKLIN Hannah	2/12		Sep		unknown
FOX John	2		Nov		dysentary
JONES Amos	63B		Apr	Laborer	erysipelas
RICHARDSON Joseph	54B		Dec	Laborer	pneumonia
RINGGOLD William	24B		Mch	Laborer	dropsy
RAISIN Milky	85B		Mch		old age
WILSON Henry	13B		Jun		fever
CORK Eliza	10B		Jan		scrofula
LAWRENCE Alfred	10/12B		Mch		consumption
JONES Marshall	11/12B		Mch		colic
WILSON Matilda	9B		May		burned
WILKINSON Margaret	17B		Sep		consumption
NICKERSON William	4		Feb		scarlet fever
RILE H C	m32	Pa	Feb		pneumonia
VANSANT William M	3/12		Mch		unknown
HAGUE Sarah C	3		Mch		scarlet fever
STOEFFER Anna	44	Ge	May		consumption
WOODLAND Samuel	41B		Nov		dropsy
MATTHEWS Sarah	5B		Nov		consumption
TURNER Siney	18B		Dec		consumption
BROWN Lina	5B		Mch		unknown
MORRIS Annie	31	Pa	Sep		cyannis
JOHNSON Isaac	19B		Jan		consumption
JOHNSON Lorenzo	4B		Apr		consumption
WILSON Perry	12B		Feb		exposure

BRICE Carrie	5		Feb		measles
JOHNSON Mary A	16B		Jan		consumption
CAMP Robert	6		Mch		scarlet fever
MOSS John	23		Jul		by machinery
RILEY Hannah	3B		Mch		whooping cough
ANDERSON Hester	3B		Mch		fever
PRISBY Alex	4B		Apr		fever
STOUTS David	60B		Jan	Laborer	exposure
PRISBY Adaline	1B		Jan		scrofula
STOOPS Mary	1B		May		scrofula
SEVERSON Thomas	38		Jan	Farmer	chronic dysentary
BUSICK Louisa	70		Nov		consumption
JONES Eliza	70		Nov		consumption
WARREN Mary	3		Feb		measles
FORD Hester	14B		Jan		childbirth
GOULD Sallie	19B		Nov		typhoid fever
CHAMBERS Sallie	12B		Oct		typhoid fever
BLAKE James	14B		Oct		typhoid fever
WILSON Henrietta	50B		Sep		consumption
DAVIS Margaret E	1B		Jan		whooping cough
JONES Mary J	50B		Mch		pneumonia
FORMAN William	40B		Feb		pneumonia
BROOKS Sarah	30B		Feb		pneumonia
TANNER Minnie	20B		Jun		hemorrhage
HOLLY Helen	57B		Apr		dropsey
BRADSHAW Emily	2B		Mch		bronchitis
DEVERICKS Shade	23B		Apr	Laborer	scarlet fever
COMEGYS Samuel	20B		Oct	Laborer	wagon ran over
DYCE Henrietta	45B		Dec		chronic dysentary
REYNOLDS James	63B		Aug	Laborer	bilious fever
GARRISON Isabel	25B		Nov	Laborer	consumption
WILSON John	12B		Jan		measles
FREEMAN Fisher	15B		Jan		measles
FREEMAN Jane	12B		Jan		measles
WRIGHT Annie M	62B		Jul		consumption
BUTTER Richard	36B		Dec		consumption
ANDERSON Annie M	6/12B		Aug		brain fever
MEDFORD Richard H	5/12B		Sep		unknown
STEWARD Hannah	30B		Sep		dropsy

DISTRICT #3 WORTON – KENT COUNTY 1870

8	THOMPSON Martha	35B m	Jun	Keeping house	heart disease
17	REALLY Laura	3	Aug		typhoid fever
18	NICHOLSON Mary	1/12	Aug		unknown
20	REED Jane	2/12	Apr		unknown
21	DENNY John	3/12	Mch		unknown
22	HOLLIDAY George	70 w	Mch	Farmer	pneumonia
24	JOHNSON George	1/12B	Jan		croup
25	WHEAT Susan A	36 w	Nov	Keeping house	measles

39	VANSANT no name	-		Mch	stillborn
47	BUCHANNAN no name	-		Aug	stillborn
56	PEARCE Ida	2B		Aug	cholera infantum
5-	BROWN Walter	3B		Jul	measles
97	HANES Daniel	69 m		Feb Farmer	consumption
116	TAYLOR Robert	5		Dec	shot by accident
117	HYNSON Samuel	22B		Jul Farm hand	consumption
134	WORMEL Ford	1B		Jul	cholera infantum
136	BECK Elwood	5/12		Jul	cholera infantum
153	MURRAY Polly	8B		Apr	measles
160	TAYLOR no name	-		Aug	stillborn
160	TAYLOR no name	-		Aug	stillborn
161	RASIN Maria	28B		Apr Domestic	congestion of bowels
234	MEEKINS Sophia	70B w		Apr	paralysis
277	OWENS William	5		Apr	burned
282	JONES Mary	39B m		Apr Keeping house	pneumonia
292	HYNSON Samuel	2/12B		Aug	cholera infantum
296	HANSON Anna	5B		Jun	paralysis
298	BROOKS Sarah	21B m		Apr Domestic	typhoid fever
296	SPRY Emily	43 m		Jun Keeping house	rheumatism
305	NICHOLSON James	40		Mch Farm hand	typhoid
317	BROWN Eugenia	1B		May	pneumonia
319	HOLLY Elanora	35B m		Jun Keeping house	lung disease
319	HOLLY John L W	1B		Feb	epilepsy
	FREEMAN William	40M m		Jan Farm hand	pneumonia
	BROOKS Sarah	35B m		May Domestic	pneumonia
	SNOWDEN Richard	58B m		Aug Farm hand	consumption

DISTRICT #4 & CHESTERTOWN - KENT COUNTY 1870

51	BROWN WALTER	11/12B		May	hydrophobia
53	BAYEN Isaac	60M m		Apr Farmer	pneumonia
58	BLAKE Sarah	31B w		May Keeping house	consumption
58	BLAKE Ann	7B		Aug	consumption
59	WRIGHT Alexander	19B		Aug	consumption
88	DWYER Gertrude	10		Mch	disease of bowel
90	COLLINS Annie	3/12		Apr	consumption
112	VOSS Mary	89 w		Feb	old age
113	MUNSON Charles	17B		Oct Farm hand	typhoid fever
12-	GREENWOOD Ellen	60 m		May Keeping house	consumption
---	HACHET Philip	1B		Oct	croup
143	RINGGOLD Anderson	42 w		Jan	typhoid fever
144	SMITH Alfred	2		Dec	croup
144	SMITH James	7/12		May	cholera infantum
181	SMITH Samuel	62 m		Jan	pneumonia
187	MURRAY Mary	11/12B		Sep	disease of brain
187	GARDNER George	37B m		Feb Farm hand	consumption
1-2	PHILLIPS James	51B m		Jun	consumption
222	MERRITT Mary	13	De	Sep	pneumonia
22-	MURRAY Kitty	50B m		May Domestic	dropsey
223	GRANGER Caroline	44B m		May Domestic	dropsey
224	BLAKE Sallie	25B m		Jun Keeping house	consumption
125	no name	-B		May	stillborn

261	DAVIS Rebecca	25B m		Jun	Keeping house	heart disease
263	FRISBY Martha	36B m		Feb		consumption
263	FRISBY Rachel	21B		Feb		pneumonia
267	CHAMBERS Lucy	1B		Sep		brain fever
293	THOMPSON Benjamin	19B		Oct	Farm hand	inflammation brain
294	ALCOTT Mary	11		Apr		pneuminia
314	SHEPARD David	72B m		Mch		pneumonia
47	BORDLEY Margaret	25B		Mch	Keeping house	consumption
47	BORDLEY Edward	4B		Sep		measles
47	BORDLEY Henry	2B		Sep		measles
50	HAYES John	26B		Sep	Farm hand	consumption
52	JOHNSON William	27B		Dec	Farm hand	brain fever
311	ASHLEY Mary	81 w		Dec		old age
311	STAUFFER Pancalius	56 m	Ba	Jan	Carpenter	dropsey
322	WILSON Mary E	2B		Jul		cholera infantum
322	WILSON William	4B		Oct		inflammation brain
326	JOHNSON Richard	2B		Apr		consumption
342	PEARCE Martha	41 w		Mch		measles
343	JONES John B	7/12M		Sep		inflammation bowel
6	WILSON Mary	46B m		Dec	Keeping house	tumor
64	WOODLAND Marie	66M m		Nov	Keeping house	pneumonia
67	GALE Hester	30M m		Nov	Keeping house	consumption
67	HOPKINS Henry	3B		May		inflammation brain
71	_____ Ann	2B		Feb		consumption
77	JACKSON Flora	6/12B		Nov		unknown
77	JACKSON Sarah	11/12B		Mch		unknown
51	FRISBY Arriminta	42M m		Jan	Keeping house	consumption
51	RASIN Dell	2B		Mch		consumption
51	RASIN Sallie	2/12B		May		consumption
51	Y___ John	_3B		May		inflammation brain
54	THOMAS Mary	3/12B		Jul		consumption
68	_____ Mary	40 m		Dec	Keeping house	measles
	_____ Ellen	13		Dec		measles
	Anne	8		Dec		measles
87	TILMAN Sarah	10B		Oct		convulsions
127	_____ Horace	70B m		Jul	Farm hand	colic
134	_____ Mary	35B m		Mch	Keeping house	pneumonia
138	DAVIS William	15		Nov		congestion of lungs
154	BENEY Matilda	50B m		Mch	Keeping house	fall
173	TURNER Deborah	68 w		May	Keeping house	congestion lungs
188	CHASE Alexander	1/12B		Aug		stillborn
188	CHASE Samuel	-B		Aug		stillborn
195	AARON Aletha	30B m		Jan	Keeping house	pneumonia
211	WILLIAMS Laura	-B		Oct		teething
226	RUSSELL Sarah	6/12B		May		cholera infantum
235	KENNEDY Rosy	50M m		Oct	Keeping house	heart disease
272	LEE Nancy	3B		Oct		brain fever
299	SPENCER Henrietta	60 w		Apr	Farming	pneumonia

3-2 _____ _____	69	m	Feb	Farm hand	pneumonia
345 _____ _____	9B		Mch	Farm hand	epilepsy
346 _____ Anna	14B		Jun		inflammation brain
402 _____ _____	f66	m	Aug		disease of uterus
407 _____ John	40	m	Sep	Farm hand	bowel disease
41- _____ _____	90	w	Mch		old age
4-- MADDOX _____	40	m	Nov	Keeping house	congestive chill
4-- SHAW Richard J	41	m	Jun	Sailor	diabetes
479 _____ _____	1/12		Feb		convulsions
497 _____ Damon B	4		Feb		typhoid fever
5-- BUCK John	72		Jun		pneumonia
5-- _____ Harriet	1/12		May		dysentary
5-- _____ _____ B	3B		Sep		measles
55- MEARS Andrew	1B		May		consumption

–	DUNBRACCO Nathan	12	Apr		scarlet fever
–	DUNBRACCO Howard	1	Apr		scarlet fever
12	EMERSON Elmira	15	Oct		typhoid fever
12	EMERSON Clement	1	Mch		typhoid fever
16	ANDERSON Mary	9	Mch		appoplexy
27	SHEETS Charles	12	Nov		consumption
27	SHEETS Hannah	26	Sep		pneumonia
42	HARTLEY Mary W	11	Mch		scarlet fever
-6	SPARKS Lilly	2	Jan		scarlet fever
-3	WALLS Walter	5	Aug		cholera infantum
14	ARMSTRONG Henry	1/12	Mch		unknown
3	WALLS Catharine	36	Mch		chronic rheumatism
72	PLATER William	62B	Dec		pneumonia
74	CAMPER Samuel	2B	Apr		pneumonia
42	WOODLAND William	36 B	Aug		disease of breast
	BROOKS Samuel	1/12B	Aug		unknown
	PRATT Bennett	46	Dec		consumption
	FELTON Elizabeth	7/12	Apr		pneumonia
244	TOWNSEND Jacob	65	May		
239	CHEW Sarah	3/12	Dec		unknown
	CHEW Laura	2	Aug		consumption
365	TRAVERS Sparks	1	May		unknown
372	PRICE Rachel	33	Dec		consumption
388	_____ John W	6-	Sep		bilious fever
433	LATON Lydia A	11	Oct		bilious fever
441	COMEGYS Edward	9/12	Jul		cholera
501	PARDEE Essie	4/12	Mch		cholera
511	M_LLY Charles	27B	May		typhoid fever
525	BORDLEY Charels	65B	Mch		pneumonia
542	WALTER G___	1B	Jun		unknown
551	TURNER Samuel	19B	Jan		burned
558	SINCLAIR ___	1/12	Mch		unknown
562	MERRICK Ezekial	42	Mch		dropsey
581	BUSH Andrew P	4	May		inflammation brain
	BUSH Sallie J	1	Aug		unknown

	DISTRICT #1 & #2 QUENN ANNE COUNTY 1870				
585	BR___ Martha	21	Sep	Seamstress	consumption
	BR___ Sallie	-/12	Feb		unknown
595	DENNIS William	55B m	Jan		consumption
595	HYNSON Mary	45B m	Apr	Housekeeper	dropsey chest
610	_____ Mary C	1	Aug		cholera infantum
611	WALLEN Mary	1/12	Apr		unknown
623	BLACKSTONE	7/12	Apr		unknown
624	H___ Peregrine	21	May	Laborer	unknown

963 BENNETT William	-/12		Aug		inflammation brain
979 BROWN William	25B m		Apr		pneumonia
980 PRICE Robert			Jun		cholera infantum
1054 CONADEN Sarah	43 m		May	Housekeeper	consumption
1061 STARKEY	-/12		Dec		unknown
1115 WELLS Charlotte	21 m		Apr	Housekeeper	consumption
1116 SMITH Martha	--B m		May		diptheria
1127 KELLY Sarah	59 m		Mch		dysentary
1146 BROWN Ann	14B		Sep	Domestic	consumption
HOLDEN John	29 m		Mch		typhoid fever
1153 BULLEN Frances	35 m		May		pneumonia
1186 MACKEY Thomas	55 m	Ir	Mch	Shoe maker	consumption
1175 JONES Catharine	65B m		Apr	Housekeeper	typhoid fever
1194 JARRETT Mollie	1/12		Jul		cholera infantum
1339 WRIGHT Mary	85B w		Apr		pneumonia
DELL Maggie	2/12		Jul		inflammation brain

DISTRICT # 3 QUENN ANN COUNTY 1870					
293 HACKET Milly	73B		Mch	Pauper	dropsey
293 JOHNSON James	58B		Apr	Pauper	consumption
293 TILGHMAN Letitia	83B		Apr	Pauper	old age
293 BROWN Les	25B		Apr	Pauper	consumption
293 LEMERICK James	73		May	Pauper	congestive chill
296 CHANCE Louisa	34 m		Sep	Housekeeper	congestive chill
300 COUNCIL Fanny	60		May		consumption
319 LANE James J	12		Aug	Student	bilious fever
333 MOFFET Salonia	1/12		Feb		diptheria
333 WRIGHT William	2		May		diptheria
333 WRIGHT Emma	2/12		May		diptheria
371 ANDERSON James	29B m		Feb	Farm hand	consumption
371 THOMAS C___	6/12B		Jul		unknown
372 DEFORD Nancy	50B		Mch	Housekeeper	pneumonia
372 DEFORD William E	19		Mch	Farm hand	typhoid fever
378 SMITH Artemus	46 m	De	Mch	Farmer	pneumonia
378 SMITH William T	18	De	Mch	Farm hand	pneumonia
422 SMITH John T	20		May	Farm hand	pneumonia
422 HENRY Charles	2B		Jun		pneumonia
422 SHENBROOKS James M	21		Apr	Carpenter	typhoid fever
422 MORGAN Laura V	6/12		Apr		measles
501 BAYNARD R C	87 m		Apr		cancer
517 BULLEN Sarah A	6/12		Jun		bowel disease
542 BORDLEY Henrietta	23 m		Aug		unknown
547 FEDDEMAN Ernest	2/12		Jul		
573 ASHCOM Thomas	86 w		Oct		old age
627 WRIGHT James H	3		Mch		typhoid fever
636 LACY Elizabeth	60 w		May	Housekeeper	consumption
660 KELLY William P	8/12		Apr		

670	BAYLEE James	50B m	Mch	Farm hand	dropsey
676	CONNOLLY Susan	67 w	Jan		consumption
692	TAYLOR Sarah A	48 w	May	House keeper	typhoid fever
708	BURNS James A	53 m	Mch	Farmer	pneumonia
775	KELLY Daniel	62B m	Apr	Farm hand	pneumonia
775	THOMAS John P	6/12	Jun		diarrhea

DISTRICT # 3   QUEEN ANN COUNTY   1870

15	JOHNS Benjamin	14B	Apr	Farm hand	consumption
41	PIKER James	25B	Apr	Farm hand	pneumonia
42	MALOY A M	62	Nov		typhoid fever
137	WILLIAMS Ellen	6/12B	Jan		
138	COMEGYS Neal	70B	Apr		
139	HENRY Malinda	4/12B	Sep		consumption
156	WELLS Mary E	16B	Feb		heart disease
160	WILSON Clair	40B m	Jan	Farm hand	consumption
161	TOLSON Reid	50 m	Apr	Farmer	typhoid fever
164	HINSON Rebecca A	54B m	May	House keeper	pneumonia
164	HINSON Margaret C	3B	Feb	House keeper	scarlet fever
164	HINSON Samuel	12B	Apr		consumption
164	HINSON Sarah R	1B	May		dysentary
177	BROOKS Clarance	1/12B	Jan		congestive chill
191	COLGAN Mary	6/12	Apr		
222	DUNNING Clara D	1	Aug		diarrhea
223	THOMAS E	1	Jul		diarrhea
223	BAILY Robert	2/12B	Aug		pneumonia
237	HARRIS Elmer	2/12	Oct		diarrhea
238	JACOBS William	25B m	Jan	Farm hand	dropsey
238	COOPER Henry H	1	Aug		dropsey
251	CHAPMAN Nancy	70	Dec		diptheria
251	EMORY Nancy	90B w	Apr		diptheria
268	HANDY James	1/12B	Mch		pneumonia
268	HANDY Albert	1/12B	Oct		pneumonia
269	MEADY Mary E	40 m	Dec	House keeper	pneumonia
269	MEADY William M	1	Dec		consumption
272	ERVING James w	14B	Aug	Farm hand	typhoid fever
274	BELL Jane	40B	Feb		typhoid fever
286	THOMAS Sally R	21B	Mch		consumption
289	MILLER Henny	60B m	May	House keeper	consumption
293	HUTCHENS Charles	40B m	Jul	Pauper	consumption
293	HAZELTON Irving	65B m	Sep	Pauper	consumption
293	COOPER Robert	90B w	Mch	Pauper	old age
293	LYNCH Elizabeth	58 m	Mch		consumption

WHITE M G	3	Jun		congestive chill
RINGGOLD Martha	20	May		consumption
NICHOLSON Benjamin	65B	Mch		apoplexy
LEGG E C	1	May		diarrhea
NICHOLSON John	30B	Feb		consumption
CREADINE Minta	27B	Feb		childbirth
MEREDITH Benjamin	5B	Dec		pneumonia
HERBERT E L	6	Oct		diarrhea
FISHER Charles	25B	Aug		pneumonia
HEATH Julia	20B	Nov		pneumonia
DAVIS Julia	56B	Jan		paralysis
GARDNER Mrs John W	23	Apr		childbirth

DISTRICT #5 QUEEN ANN COUNTY 1870

	DELLAHAY Annie C	1 3/12	Feb		pneumonia
	CONYER Rebecca	85B	Apr		rheumatism
	CONYER Wm Henry	4/12B	Jul		cholera infantum
	JOHNSON Henrietta	3/12B	Jul		cholera infantum
	BOWSER Henrietta	97B w	Jun		apoplexy
	SIMERS Mary J	35B	Feb		acute rheumatism
	HIGGENS Mary A	72 w	Aug		paralysis
146	WATKINS John W	2B	May		measles
144	GOULD Betsie	1B	Jul		measles
155	SINGLE Henry	75B w	Dec	Domestic	
152	BROWN Elizabeth	9/12B	Dec		unknown
157	DAVIDSON Marcella	23B m	Aug	Keeping house	consumption
179	SMALLWOOD Lazarie	3B	Aug		burned
183	SIMMERS Henry	17B	Aug	Farm laborer	consumption
186	MANSFIELD Robert	4/12	Aug		cholera infantum
188	SHERWOOD F A	f53 m	Feb	Keeping house	unknown
191	IRSSELTON Thomas	24 m	Sep	Farmer	pneumonia
192	GRIFFIN Henrietta M	55	Feb	Teacher	cancer
192	GRIFFIN Julia W	59	Feb		consumption
198	THOMAS Isabella	11/12	Sep		whooping cough
201	DAWSON Agnes R	1 9/12	Jun		cholera infantum
219	FREEMAN Louisa	12B	May	Domestic	unknown

11	COOPER George	12		Nov	attends school	typhoid fever
20	PARKER Anna	1		Jun		cholera infantum
32	PUSEY Martha	30 m		Feb	Keeping house	consumption
49	DENNNIS Spencer Jr	24B		Jun	Farm laborer	consumption
71	MARSHALL Tamar	55B m		Nov	Keeping house	remittant fever
72	TILGHMAN Sarah	15B		Mch	Domestic	pneumonia
72	TILGHMAN Sarah H	1/12B		Mch		unknown
72	TILGHMAN Esther	1/12B		Mch		unknown
96	PUSEY Noah	1B		Apr		pneumonia
96	PUSEY Willaim	4B		Jul		pneumonia
109	LANKFORD John L	43 m		Sep	Farmer	gout
130	ELSEY Ellen	27B m		May	House keeper	consumption
132	DORMAN Ann	30B m		May	House Keeper	pneumonia
156	HICKMAN George	68 w	Va	Feb	Farmer	pneumonia
159	BOSMAN Wesley	1		Feb		dispepsia
160	NELSON William	1		Nov		diptheria
165	McALLISTER Joseph	2		Jul		inflammation bowel
166	DALE James	4		Apr		consumption
183	KING Charles	3		Sep		diptheria
213	FOOKS Sallie	46B m		Mch	Keeping house	consumption
228	ROBERTS Henry	10B		Jul		dropsey stomach
230	POLLIT William	1B		Jul		remittant fever
274	KING Ida	1B		Sep		cholera infantum
275	BETHARD Susan	35 m		Jan		puerperal fever
288	JOHNSON Rosa	45B m		Apr	Keeping house	consumption
290	HASTING Edwin	1		Apr		cholera infantum
300	HITCH John	1B		Jan		pneumonia
325	FONTAIN Joseph	1		Oct		cholera infantum
374	PORTER Alpheus	2		Nov		diptheria
374	PORTER CHLORENA	4		Nov		diptheria
380	NEWMAN Henny	23B m		Aug		consumption
405	DUFFY Mary	1B		Jun		whooping cough
405	DUFFY Sallie	1B		Jul		whooping cough
405	DUFFY Biddy	24B m		Jul	House Keeper	consumption
422	CULLEN Emily	1		Jul		cholera infantum
441	HEATH Elijah	65 w	NJ	May	Farmer	fractured leg
445	HAYMAN Samuel M	27		Dec	Blacksmith	cancer
509	TYLER Williamanna	3		Jan		diptheria
612	JONES Samuel W	67 m		Sep	Farmer	suicide/cut throat
620	CHETAN Elizabeth A	33 m		Sep	Keeping house	dispepsia
620	CHETAN Robert R	10/12		Jul		cholera infantum
639	DASHIELL Cara	1B		Mch		dysentary
658	CROCKET Ann	30 w		Mch	Keeping house	consumption
662	McGRATH Mary	50B m		Mch	Keeping house	consumption
683	HANDY Mary	85B w		Apr		old age
	ABBOTT Mason	87 w		Jul		old age
	ABBOTT Charles	50		Sep		manic
	PATTERSON Catherine	26	ffb	Jun		consumption
	PATTERSON Helen	66 m		Sep	Keeping house	breast cancer

10	PATTERSON Sarah	48B m		May	Domestic	rheumatism
13	NEWMAN Thomas	1/12		Mch		hydrocephalus
25	PHABRIA Thomas	77 m		Nov	Farmer	bilious fever
36	ROBERTSON Lizzie	9/12		Dec		whooping cough
91	BEDSWORTH Emily	1		Dec		consumption
129	WALLACE Molly	1		Jul		typhoid fever
140	CURTIS Sarah	5/12B		Jan		diptheria
158	JONES John	35 m		Apr	Farmer	consumption
163	WILKENS Eveline	27		Oct	Keeping house	consumption
173	KELLY Mary	1		Apr		whooping cough
178	DAVIS Arthur	82		Apr	Farmer	old age
181	HOWARD Henry	1		May		typhoid fever
193	JONES Pringle	1B		Jan		typhoid fever
207	LORD Ellen	74 w		Feb	Keeping house	consumption
244	WHITE Thomas	44 m		Mch	Waterman	consumption
	WALLER Sally	65B w		May	Keeping house	consumption

BRINKLEYS DISTRICT - SOMERSET COUNTY 1870

3	COULBOURNE Arianna	16B		Aug		measles
13	TURPEN Hester	62B m		Aug	Housekeeper	heart disease
39	ADAMS Jane	74 w		Mch		old age
42	TARLOW Ida E	1		Oct		diarrhea
44	HORSEY Zipporah	60 m		Jun		billious fever
61	KEARSEY Hamet	27B		May	Domestic	consumption
61	WHITTINGTON Wm A	1B		Jun		measles
66	CONNER Iowa C	2		Sep		whooping cough
67	WHITTINGTON John	16B		Apr	Sailor	drowned
102	JOHNSON Smith	9/12B		Jan		headfall
116	JOHNSON Mary J	3B		Feb		burned to death
116	JOHNSON Washington	1B		Aug		thrush
118	ROUNDS Matilda J	3/12B		Feb		croup
124	OUTEN John Henry	22B		Mch	Farm laborer	typhoid fever
135	DRYDEN Robert L	55 m		Nov	Farmer	apoplexy
142	HULL John C	60B m		May	Sailor	heart disease
154	HORSEY Levin	85B w		Aug	Farmer	typhoid fever
166	SCOTT Mary G	10		Feb		pneumonia
172	MATTHEWS William	77 m		Apr	Farmer	erysipelas
179	BRIDDELL A_____	m1/12		Dec		headfall
193	EWELL Charles	6/12		Jan		croup
209	WARREN Mary E	6/12	Pa	Oct		indigestion
224	WHITTINGTON George	1/12		Feb		headfall
228	LANKFORD Aaron A	1		Jul		dysentary
246	HOWETH William	74 m		Jul	Farmer	typhoid fever
248	BELL Harriet A	14B		Apr		intermittant fever
251	BELL Laurrinda	3B		Aug		measles
251	BELL Charles H	2B		Aug		measles
255	DIXON Anna	21		Jun		pneumonia

269	BALLARD A_____	1/12B	Jan		headfall
273	MAGDALINA Magdalina	5	Mch		diptheria
275	CANNON Elword	1	Oct		diptheria
303	CRISP Martha B	9/12	Feb		pneumonia
332	DAVIS Willis L	1	Dec		quinsey
337	ADAMS Elizabeth J	6	Jan		diptheria
337	ADAMS Louisa	2	Feb		erysipelas
347	LAMBDEN Theodore	20	Nov	Sailor	typhoid fever
365	WILKENS Louisa	20 m	Oct	House keeper	puerperal fever
367	HOLLAND Louisiana	27 m	Apr	House keeper	puerperal fever
384	STURGIS E J	f28	Jun		convulsions
384	H____ Ida	13	Sep		typhoid fever
401	MILBOURNE Caleb	12B	Jul		typhoid fever
401	MILBOURNE Emily	4B	Sep		typhoid fever
402	SWIFT Henry	60 m	Mch	Farmer	pneumonia
412	BALLARD John	60B m	Jul	Farm laborer	kidney disease
431	DAVIS Mary E	26 m	Jan	House keeper	inflammation brain
444	ROBINSON Pricilla A	4/12	Sep		consumption
455	ATKINSON Edward W	1/12	May		unknown

	DUBLIN DISTRICT - SOMERSET COUNTY 1870				
1	MATTHEWS William	75 m	Apr	Farmer	consumption
7	OUTEN Charlotte	45B m	Nov	Keeping house	consumption
90	WILLIAMS Mary	42B m	Dec	Keeping house	typhoid fever
90	WILLIAMS Sarah	20B	Dec	Domestic	inflammation brain
90	WILLIAMS Harriet	13B	Dec	Domestic	diptheria
133	WILLIAMS Charity	70B w	Apr	Keeping house	consumption
148	WILSON Lavina	30B w	Dec	Domestic	pneumonia
154	HAYWARD Leah	80B w	Feb		old age
165	HAYWARD Frank	3B	Oct		paralysis
175	MILES Maria	45B m	Jan	Keeping house	inflammation brain
200	MILLA Lanny	3/12	Mch		whooping cough
230	DRYDEN Eliza	62 m	Apr	Keeping house	inflammation brain

	HUNGRY NECK DISTRICT - SOMERSET COUNTY 1870				
	GIBBS Jane	40	Oct		remittant fever
	Tobe	22B	Jan		consumption
	HARGIS James	55B w	Mch		pneumonia
	Kite	45B	Apr		consumption
	ELSEY Gusta	22B	May		consumption
	DARBY Mitcha	6/12	Apr		whooping cough
49	HOLLAND Sarah	9	Aug		remittant fever
50	WILLIAMS Peter	35 m	Feb	Waterman	pneumonia
75	HARRIS Delia	28 w	Dec	House keeping	consumption
100	WEBSTER Kate	8/12	Mch		inflammation brain
104	STREET Mary	12	Oct	at school	tyhoid fever
143	JONES Lester	2	May		whooping cough
144	SCOTT Mary	5	May		whooping cough
148	MURREL Sally	40 w	Oct	Keeping house	consumption
139	AUSTIN John	70 m	Aug	Waterman	consumption

20	COX Alijah B	1	Aug		measles/wh cough
28	BEAUCHAMP Theodore	1	Jul		cholera infantum
30	BEAUCHAMP Charles	24 m	Mch	Sailor	typhoid fever
52	DICE Pricilla A	9/12	Jan		hydrophobia
70	LANDON Larabee	73 m	Jul	Sailor	scrofula
95	MADDOX James	14B	Jul	Farm laborer	inflammation bowel
96	MILES Leah C	1/12B	Jan		dropsey of brain
98	WASHINGTON Francis H	3/12B	Aug		whooping cough
113	BALLARD George H W	2B	Jul		measles
158	HALL Elijah L	43 m	Dec	ret Merchant	consumption
176	JOHNSON Pricilla	2B	Dec		teething
197	MADDOX Daniel	3B	Aug		diptheria
198	WATERS Rosa	46 w	Jun		chronic dyspepsia
198	SMITH Sarah	62	Sep		consumption
210	Maddox Ida	1/12	Feb		headfall
247	HARVEY William J	1B	May		cholera infantum
247	HARVEY Sarah C	1B	May		cholera infantum
252	LONG Sarah E	9/12	Dec		whooping cough
253	CARNE Laura J	2	Aug		remittant fever
254	REESE George W	1	Aug		teething
264	SMITH Maria	30B m	Apr	House keeping	consumption
266	HULL John	70B m	Aug	Sailor	dropsey chest
274	DORSEY Laura F	4/12	May		unknown
272	MADDOX Sally	60	May		consumption
	LEATHERBERRY Samuel	35B m	Mch	Sailor	typhoid fever
	MILES Ann M	6B	Apr		typhoid fever
	HAYWARD Charles	55B m	Apr		dropsey of chest
279	SCOTT Sarah A	55 w	Jul	House keeping	dyspepsia
280	STEWART Ann	40B w	May	Domestic	typhod fever
289	WILSON Henry A	2M	Aug		cholera infantum
302	CURTIS Mary a	19B	Dec		consumption
314	COULBOURNE Benjamin	7/12B	May		convulsions
330	LANDON Arintha	16	Aug		intermittant fever

SMITH ISLAND DISTRICT - SOMERSET COUNTY 1870

56	MARSH John F	6/12	Aug		chronic diarrhea
61	BRADSHAW Hambleton	83 w	Sep		old age/dibility
50	MISTER Mary H	21 m	Oct	House keeping	typhoid fever

LAWSON DISTRICT - SOMERSET COUNTY 1870

8	CROWELL Sala A	1	Sep		dysentary
9	HANDY David	80B w	Apr	Surveyor	heart disease
11	BENSON Rosetta	2B	Aug		chronic diarrhea
22	WYATT James C	4/12	Jul		measles
46	WALKER John C	77M m	Nov	Sailor	asthma
52	STEVENSON Alice	6/12	Sep		dysentary
55	ROACH Susan A	30B m	Mch	Keeping house	pleurisy
55	ROACH Mary E	6/12B	Mch		thrush
63	RIGGEN Mary	78 w	Jun	Keeping house	paralysis

65	SANDSBURY John W	64 w	Jan	Carpenter	typhoid fever
66	DAUGHERTY Emmeline	F11/12	Sep		inflammation brain
76	RIGGINS George E	1	Mch		teething
86	WARD Susan W	41 m	Jun	Keeping house	consumption
132	FISHER Robert L	3/12	Jun		pneumonia
134	ROBBINS Mary A	40 m	Oct	Keeping house	consumption
145	EVANS George B	14	Jun	Sailor	kidney disease
159	JOHNSON Haney E	25	Feb		consumption
172	WARD Jane	1B	Dec		nerves
181	LANGHARTY Jacob	26 m	Jan	Sailor	killed in the ___
202	MUIR Lucy e	1	Aug		whooping cough
183	DISE George	45 m	Dec	Sailor	consumption
215	BURTON Levin	40B m	Aug	Farm laborer	remittant fever
216	STEVENSON Lovey	17B	Apr		burned to death
232	GRIFFIN Sarah C	19B m	Sep	House keeping	billious fever
244	ADAMS Rufus A	1	Aug		dysentary
257	JOHNSON George T	30	Nov	Farmer	consumption
291	CURTIS Harrison R	9/12B	Sep		dropsey of brain
316	LANKFORD Agnes M	26 m	Aug	Keeping house	typhoid fever
318	WARD Aisa	6/12	Jul		cholera infantum
337	BETSWORTH John B	72 m	Apr	Brickmaker	dropsey bowel
347	STERLING William a	2/12	Nov		dropsey of brain
357	STERLING Thomas	47 m	Mch	Carpenter	consumption
360	Sterling William B	23B	Jan	Sailor	pneumonia
363	McHAILL Charles W	5/12B	Feb		consumption
382	STERLING Christopher J	24	Sep	Sailor	consumption
388	STERLING Elijah	74 m	Dec	Farmer	acute rheumatism
423	STERLING Traverse	68 m	Jul	Oysterman	typhoid fever
435	MILES Henry	30B	Mch	Farm Laborer	pneumonia
442	NELSON Clara V	2	Oct		croup
468	MASON William H	44 m	Feb	Oysterman	consumption
487	MISTER Wiley D	1	May		convulsions
505	BIRD Edwin J	1	Oct		dyspepsia
515	TYLER Margaret	47 m	Mch	Keeping house	consumption
515	LAWSON Phoebe	1	Sep		chronic diarrhea
537	TARAS Clement A	1	Sep		chronic diarrhea
537	LAWSON George W	1	Dec		croup
547	LAWSON Isaac	50 m	Apr	Oysterman	cancer of mouth
556	BETSWORTH Mary E J	2	Jun		chronic diarrhea
564	BLADES James	17	Jul	Farm laborer	typhoid fever
600	COLLINS Milcah	70	Dec		typhoid fever

TANGIER DISTRICT - SOMERSET COUNTY 1870

4	WRIGHT Charlotte	6/12B	Mch		pneumonia
5	WRIGHT Hetty	45B m	Sep	Keeping house	childbirth
5	WRIGHT David	16B	Mch	Waterman	asthma
6	PRICE Ann	1B	Jul		cholera infantum
36	REED Calvin	2B	Aug		cholera infantum
38	WALLACE Lizzie	3B	Mch		pneumonia
103	THOMAS Lavinia	2	Sep		diptheria
104	HARRIS Louisa	85 w	Apr		old age

121	ROWE Molly	1		Jul		measles
146	HARRIS Lavinia	1		Aug		dysentary
147	ALBERT Ida	2		Sep		dysentary
154	BENTON Benjamin	2		Nov		measles
158	WHITE Emma	1B		Aug		cholera infantum
163	WINDSOR John	1		Feb		whooping cough
163	WINDSOR Arianna	17		Mch		consumption
197	ABBOT Luther	3		Jul		cholera infantum
199	RIDER Noah	49	m	Nov	Physician	mania
214	THOMAS Arianna	18	m	Mch	Keeping house	puerperal fever
225	WEBSTER John	36	m	Apr	Waterman	consumption

3	GREENE Mary	20B m		Mch	Domestic	pneumonia
11	SMITH Levin	56B m		May	Farm laborer	asthma
19	TOWERS Jeremiah	8		Feb	at school	inflammation brain
34	CATSCOTT Stephen	70 w	De	Jun	Farmer	paralysis
34	CATSCOTT Martha	23 m		Jul	Keeping house	consumption
48	SHANNAHAN Lizzie	27 m		Jul	Keeping house	consumption
48	JACKSON George W	3/12B		Jul		unknown
50	DUNCAN Elizabeth	81	Pa	Mch	at home	old age
57	CONOLLY Martha	-B		Feb		unknown
57	CONOLLY Mary	-B		Feb		unknown
74	PARKER Anderson	78 w	De	Feb	at home	chronic dysentary
75	TOWERS Anderson			Dec		
81	GOLDSBOROUGH Samuel R 55			Nov	at home	epileptic
91	SUTTON Henry	73B w		May		old age
94	COOPER Henry	39B		Mch		dropsey heart
109	CROSS Henry	11/12		May		scarlet fever
112	DULIN Reuben	83		Oct		burned to death
147	COOPER Henry	30B m		Mch		dropsey heart
154	BOWERS Rebecca	45 w		Feb		pleurisy & pneomonia
185	ELLIOTT Daniel	52B w		May	Farm laborer	rheumatic heart
190	name unknown	0/12		May		unknown
200	HUETT Emily	40B m		Mch	Domestic	dropsey
200	name unknown	1/12B		May		infant unknown
205	PLUMMER Mary E	11/12		Jul		brain fever
218	JONES Fanny	62B		Mch	Domestic	apoplexy
222	SPENSE Martha	35 m		Sep		childbirth
239	GRIFFIN Loftun	9/12		Jul		inflammation ____
245	VINEY William	11B		Mch		pneumonia
252	JOHNSON William	5/12B		Feb		unknown
252	JOHNSON Hester	1B		Mch		whooping cough
257	FLOYD Isaac	2B		Sep		fever
274	CLAYTON Mella	2B		Aug		unknown
277	DULIN Samuel	1/12		Jun		unknown
278	JONES Nannie	5B		Mch		pneumonia
284	JOHNSON Bennie	6B		Jun		unknown
305	CARROL Mary E	9/12		May		whooping cough
447	WOOLEN Jacob	6		Apr		killed ____
453	ROBERTS Adaline	9B		Oct		burned to death
453	ROBERTS Mary	28B m		Oct	domestic	burned to death
460	JOHNSON Sarah	24		Dec	Domestic	dyspepsia
463	MANDRIL Frances	30 m		Dec	House keeper	pneumonia
463	MANDRIL Eleanor	1/12		Jun		unknown
467	RAY Caroline	28		Aug	House Keeper	typhoid fever

2	HUGHES Matilda	2/12B		Jun		unknown
4	GREENE William	1/12B		Sep		unknown
11	GREEN Mary C	10/12B		Jul		unknown
26	BASTICK Samuel M	33 m	De	Dec	Blacksmith	accidently shot self
37	POTTER Henry	1B		Dec		teething
45	NICHOLS Sarah	1/12B		Sep		unknown
70	WILSON Mary	57 m	De	Feb		tumor
74	SONSAL Mary	36 m		Nov		puerperal fever
78	BONSAL James	1		Oct		unknown
120	COONEY Sarah	4/12	ffb	Jun		cholera infantum
127	COONEY Joseph F	5/12	ffb	Jul		cholera infantum
137	BREEZE James A	1B		Apr		took med by mistake
147	SMITH Rebecca	41 m		Dec	Keeping house	childbirth
149	LOVEDAY Elizabeth	54 m		Aug	Keeping house	dysentary
159	WRIGHTSON Frank	8/12B		Aug		inflammation brain
163	LLOYD Isaac	88B m		Feb		old age
163	HENRY Horace	1/12B		Jun		unknown
169	BANTUM Ida	3B		Feb		consumption
171	SMITH Perry	9/12B		Jun		dropsey
173	SCOTT John	1/12B		Mch		pneumonia
180	CHUZMAN George W	9/12		Jun		unknown
228	GOLT Sarah C	24 m		May		consumption
230	STEWART Josephine	1B		Sep		unknown
238	SHRIEVE Thomas J	33 m		Apr		consumption
239	CHAMBERLAIN Samuel	21		Apr		consumption
241	name unknown	1/24		May		unknown
247	LANE Edward	4/12		Jun		cholera infantum
268	GRACE James H			Apr	Merchant	inflammation stomach
278	DEMMING Mary A	17		Jun	Domestic	typhoid fever
294	BRYAN Julia	59B m		May	Domestic	tumor
296	GROOME Peregrine	76 m		May	General agent	old age
300	CAMPBELL Levin H	48 m		Nov	Druggist	pneumonia
303	SMILER Polly	16B		Jul	Domestic	consumption
307	COLLISON William S	37 m		Sep	Carpenter	acute diarrhea
312	BENNY William J	1/12		Jun		unknown
324	MATTHEWS Thomas	24 m		Jul	Cabinet maker	drowned
334	KENNARD Elizabeth	62 w		Feb	at home	inflammation bowel

DISTRICT #2 - TALBOT COUNTY 1870					
3	LAURANCE James	26B	Jun	Farm laborer	consumption
4	MURRY Virginia	1B	Jul		whooping cough
18	MANAKY Martha	52 m	Jan	Keeping house	pneumonia
22	DENNY Wilbur F	21	Jul	Farm laborer	congestive chills
34	WILLIAMS Maria	2/12B	Sep		
50	YOUNG Samuel H	17B	Sep		
53	JACKSON E A	f33	Dec	Keeping house	consumption

53	JACKSON Edwin	8/12		Jul		cholera infantum
56	GREEN Oliver	33B	m	Oct	Farm laborer	consumption
7-	MELLY Ellen	9B		Sep		typhoid fever
88	LEONARD Elizabeth	24		Nov		consumption
92	KIRK Milla	-/12		Aug		cholera infantum
94	AUDEN Clara	44	m	Oct	Farming	consumption
96	ROSS Maria	6/12B		Apr		
114	VALIANT ____	f33	m	Jun	Keeping house	consumption
11-	CHANEY Thomas	53M	m	Jan	Farm laborer	consumption
123	HOBBS Thomas H	36	m	Nov	Farm laborer	consumption
126	CARPENTER Mary	19		Jan		cattarrh
131	MARSHALL Frances A	30		Jan		consumption
131	HARRISON Ann C	19		Jan		consumption
137	____ ____	1/12B				spasm
138	GIBSON Mary	-B		May		cholera infantum
144	MULLIKEN John		m	Dec	Farm laborer	consumption
144	MELVIN Eliza	67	m	Feb	Keeping house	rheumatic fever
177	KILLMAN Levi	11/12		Aug		whooping cough
217	SHERWOOD Robert	14		Aug	Farmlaborer	inflammation ____
219	DALE Mary A	4		Jan		measles
219	DALE Eleanora	1		Jun		cholera infantum
227	CHASE ____	m68	m	May	Sailor	pneumonia
233	PALMER Lewis	34M	m	Jul	Farm laborer	consumption
242	JACKSON Sidney	3/12B		Jan		cold
244	CAULK Caroline	26		Mch		consumption
246	THOMPSON Benjamin	3B		Jan		cholera infantum
246	THOMPSON Josephine	1B		Sep		cholera infantum
247	MARSHALL Margaret	28	m	Nov		consumption
250	COOPER Thomas	30	m	Jun	Farmer	consumption
263	CARROLL Thomas R	53	m	Jul	Farmer	hydrophobia
270	LARRIMORE Robert	36	m	Apr	Farm laborer	pneumonia
283	LARRIMAORE Thomas	35		Mch	Oysterman	____ exposure
284	WAYMAN Lucretia	60	w	Jan	Keeping house	pneumonia
294	BUDGES Lydia J	20	m	Sep	Keeping house	consumption
303	____ James E	22		Feb	Farm laborer	consumption
311	HARRISON Thomas	73	m	Jan	Farmer	heart disease
330	THOMAS William	43B	m	Oct	Farm laborer	consumption
330	THOMAS Powell	14B		Apr	Farm laborer	consumption
341	ROLLE Mary	54	w	Apr	Keeping house	pneumonia
347	OREM Nicholas	70	w	Oct	Farmer	consumption
347	BLADES Louisa	34		Mch		consumption
373	WHEATON Henrietta	43	m	May	Keeping house	dyspepsia
379	GRAHAM Julia A	77	w	May		bilious cholic
390	NEWMAN James	62	m	Mch		hydrophobia
403	TARBUTTON John	3/12		Mch		cattarrh
412	FORD Martha	1/12		Oct		influenza
412	FORD Caroline	1/12		Oct		influenza

426	____ George M	24		NY	Sep	Druggist	consumtion
443	SKINNER Ruth	91 w			Mch		old age
447	MATTHEW Thomas H	27 m			Jul	Cabinet maker	drowned
465	FAIRBANK Lydia E	2			Mch		pneumonia
463	TAN John	36 m			Jul	Oysterman	chronic bronchitis
484	COVEY Susan	59 m			Dec	Keeping house	pneumonia
494	FREELAND Samuel A	4			Mch		
497	____ Julia	78B w			Jan	Keeping house	pneumonia
518	HARRINGTON Mary	71			Jan		dyspepsia
528	HAMBLETON Albert	1			Aug		cholera infantum
578	HARRISON Arthur	19			Aug	at school	typhoid fever
549	THOMAS Elizabeth	32B m			Aug	Keeping house	typhoid fever
550	BRADLEY John H	3			Jul	at home	typhoid fever
551	CORNISH Charles H	5B			Jun	at home	typhoid fever
562	CHANCE William F	4/12			Jul	at home	cholera infantum
566	JENKINS Amanda	1/12			Nov	at home	inflammation lungs
570	JESTER William	56 m			Feb	Farmer	paralysis
589	HOLLIDAY Rosetta	4/12B			Aug	at home	cholera infantum
591	HUGHLETT Jeanette	24B m			Oct	Keeping house	inflammation stomach
600	THOMAS Anna	60 m			Aug	Keeping house	liver disease
603	LEE Robert W	10/12			Sep	at home	cholera infantum
604	FLANNIGAN Andrew	70 m			Jun	Ship builder	enlargement liver
627	DICKENSON Lambert	26B			Aug	Farm laborer	pneumonia
635	BANTOM Rebecca	50B m			Jan	Keeping house	pneumonia
635	BANTOM Rebecca F	7B			May	at home	pneumonia

DISTRICT #3 - TALBOT COUNTY 1870

6	GAMBREL Anna M	30 w		May	Keeping house	spotted fever
12	ADAMS Jane	20M m		Aug	Domestic	dropsey
29	FAULKNER William B	29 m		Dec	Farmer	typhoid fever
28	AYRES Mary	48 m		Mch		consumption
53	PASTERFIELD Fannie	1		Jul		spotted fever
53	MACKEY Rosa	110B m		Apr		old age
59	HANDY Margaret	35M m		Mch		consumption
61	MILLER Chester	62B m		Jun		pneumonia
61	MILLER Mary	14		Aug		pneumonia
58	KIRBY Almira	1B		Jul		inflammation bowel
63	FOX Hannah C	1		Aug		inflammation bowel
70	BLAKE Martha M	5		Mch		spotted fever
72	MERRICK Sarah A	45 m		Jan	Keeping house	spotted fever
73	MOORE Vincent	90B w		May	Pauper	old age
73	HARRISON Charles	10		May		spotted fever
73	HENNESSE Elizabeth	44		May		consumption
73	SLAUGHTER Sarah	70B w		Aug		consumption
73	HOBBS Thomas	50 m		Nov		
73	CORNISH George	25B m		Apr		consumption
73	EARLE Elizabeth	35B m		May		consumption
73	MYRES Jeremiah	60B m		May	Pauper	old age
91	NEWNAM Margaret R	2/12		Aug	at home	cholera infantum
98	PRICE John	75B m		Mch		old age

107	DULIN Eliza A	43	m		Nov		spotted fever
122	STREETS Laura	9			Jul	at home	spotted fever
130	BEALL Margaret E	36	m		Aug	Keeping house	cancer
130	BEALL Elizabeth S	4		DC	Jul		brain disease
131	STEWART Samuel	9/12			Oct		cholera infantum
137	REYNOLD Fannie	1			Oct		diptheria
152	WILLIS Mary	26			Aug	Keeping house	consumption
180	BALL Ida	1/12			Oct	at home	unknown
227	PARROTT Annie	35	m		Jul	at home	consumption
232	MULLIKEN Minnie S	6/12			May		inflammation brain
240	CLARK Minnie	6/12			Nov		inflammation brain
	STEWART Alexander	35		Va	Jul	RR worker	sunstroke
262	GOSSAGE Mary M	8/12			Jul	at home	cholera infantum
265	HARDCASTLE Addison Y	23			Jun	Law student	consumption
268	NEWNAM Elizabeth W	57	w		Nov	Keeping house	consumption
270	HAMSLY Lillian D	1			Aug		chronic cough
279	JEFFERSON Mollie V	6/12			Jul		cholera infantum
284	STEVENS Lawrence E	6/12			Nov		cholera infantum
292	NICHOLS Mary E	41	m		Jul	Keeping house	consumption
293	CROCKETT Willimina	3			Jul		diptheria
294	WARNER Alice	18B			Jul	at home	consumption
302	GOSSAGE Richard	69	m		Feb		heart disease
302	GOSSAGE John W	2			May		diptheria
340	GLANDEN Ann Mrs	57	m		Apr	Keeping house	pneumonia
247	SLOW James T	9M			Mch		spotted fever
271	BARTLETT Richard W	11/12			Aug		cholera infantum
383	YOUNG Georgeanna	2B			Jan		spotted fever
387	EASON Anna	40	m		May	Keeping house	pneumonia
387	EASON Thomas	55	m		Mch	Farmer	erysipelas
391	ROBINSON Solomon	14			Jul	Farm laborer	spotted fever
395	ANDREW Jane	1			Aug		cholera infantum
398	MESSEX George H	4			Feb		spotted fever
402	DAVIS Thomas R	63	m		Nov	Farm laborer	consumption
407	SPARKLIN Clara	8			Apr		dropsey
437	MARTIN Nicholas	85	w	(1870)	Jun	Farmer	paralysis
439	WARREN Annie E	11			Jun	school	scarlet fever
439	WARREN Bradford H	5			Jun	school	scarlet fever
450	SAUNDERS James	65	m		Mch	Farm laborer	ruptured hernia
462	BESSEX Caroline	60B			Oct	home	old age
485	REED Margaret A	54	m		May	Keeping house	typhoid fever
492	GRIFFIN Rebecca	60	w		May	at home	pneumonia
493	GRIFFIN John E	3			Oct		diptheria
496	FLOYD Martha J	28	m		Jun	Keeping house	pneumonia
498	VALIANT Lelah V	3/12			Jul		cholera infantum
505	MINUS Augusta	2		USSR	May		unknown
531	JAMES Medford	7/12			Oct		unknown
546	WALLACE Isaiah	22B			Jun	Farm laborer	spotted fever

9	FORMAN James H	2			Jul	cholera infantum
48	MORGAN Mary	64	w		Feb	Keeping house	inflammation liver
61	NEIGHBORS James S	45	m		Mch		pleurisy
66	PERKINS Perry	75B			Feb		paralysis
66	PERKINS Aaron	1B			Feb		unknown
67	WRIGHT Alexander	23B			Apr	Farm laborer	consumption
67	WOOLFORD Lucy	5B			May		consumption
71	PERKINS Rosella	1/12M			Feb		unknown
75	name unknown	1/12B			Dec		strangled to death
81	ROSS Henry	72	w	De	Apr		rheumatism
83	CHRISTOPHER Sarah	1/12			Jun		unknown
87	JOHNSON Ennals	52	m	De	Apr		dropsey
101	PARROTT Susan	5/12			Jul		unknown
125	MATTHEWS Edward	1			Jan		catarrh fever
133	FRAMPTON Risdon	51	m		Mch		pneumonia
134	GREEN James H	58	m	De	Mch		pneumonia
162	MALONEY Ella	1/12B			Aug		unknown
166	FIPS Nelson	53	m		Apr		consumption
172	McCONIGAN Teresa	1/12			Apr		whooping cough
183	WILLSON Bascom	12B			Jan		pleurisy
184	PLATER Haorace	19B			May		pneumonia
186	COVEY Bascom	10			Jun		drowned
198	WARNER Louisa	28B	m		Dec	Keeping house	consumption
200	WILLIAMS Charles	1/12B			Jul		unknown
213	GADD Thomas H	11/12			May		whooping cough
233	QUIMBY William P	45	m		Mch		pneumonia
245	PARMER Caroline	5		NJ	Jul		typhoid fever
246	FAVINGER Mary	16		Pa	Aug		typhoid fever
259	JOHNSON Tenny	70B	m		Aug	Gardener	intermittant fever
264	BOONE Charity V	1			May	at home	lung disease
290	TARBUTTON James	60	w		Mch	Farmer	cancer
330	THOMAS Henry	67B	m		Aug	Farm laborer	dropsey
330	LUCAS Gracy	100B	w		Sep	at home	old age
330	THOMAS James	1B			Sep		consumption
347	HASSET Samuel	56	w		Mch	Carpenter	pneumonia
349	PARMER Mary	3			May		catarrh
350	REDMAN Mary A	2/12M			May		cholera infantum
352	BERNS Washington	60	m		Feb	Farmer	pneumonia
353	SEWELL Sarah E	3			Jul		cholera infantum
358	McQUAY Sallie	22B			Aug	at home	consumption
365	RUSSUM Francis E	58	m		Dec	Farmer	consumption
366	KIRBY Benjamin	73	w		Dec		old age
386	BROOKS Rhoda	30B			Jun	Keeping house	congestive chill
386	BROOKS Mary E	5B			Oct		congestive chill
411	CALLAHAN Rebecca	56	m		Feb	Keeping house	pneumonia
424	HOUSTON Hester A	24	m		Sep	Keeping house	billious
436	KELLY Ann	30	m		Sep	Keeping house	intermittant fever

444	IRELAND Rebecca	26			Sep		congestive chill
455	MINNER Sarah	13	m	De	Sep		congestive chill
455	MINNER Wilbert	1			Mch		teething

DISTRICT #5 - TALBOT COUNTY   1870

1	MARSHALL James	32			Dec		liver disease
2	HADAWAY Mary E	41	m		Jun		consumption
9	KINNEMON Josephine	27	m		Aug		measles
17	CUMMING Harry C	1			Aug		acute dysentary
17	CUMMING E E	6/12			Oct		acute dysentary
11	HARRISON Francis	2			Oct		croup
23	ROWE Ellen	18			Jul		typhoid fever
34	LOWARY James A	1			Jun		whooping cough
56	LOWE William	26			Nov	Engineer	acute dysentary
69	SEARS Julia	3			Jul		acute dysentary
69	SEARS John	10/12			Jul		acute dysentary
85	SINCLAIR Richard	1			Nov		whooping cough
85	SINCLAIR Sarah	18	m		Nov		pneumonia
121	SAYFIELD Sallie	18			Jun		consumption
123	NEELY Ellen D	23		Pa	Mch	Horse doctor	dropsey of chest
159	BAKER William	1			Mch		inflammation brain
186	COOPER Wilson	1/12B			Dec		cold
187	WRIGHTSON Jane	49	m		Jan	Keeping house	pneumonia
194	SMITH Martha	23B			Nov	Domestic	consumption
200	CAULK Kemp R	44	m		Oct	Blacksmith	pneumonia
202	SMITH William	2			Dec		dyspepsia
217	BAILY Julia	56			Mch		typhoid fever
218	PARMER Susan	1/12B			Mch		unknown
219	WRIGHTSON Ellen	42	m		Mch	Keeping house	pneumonia

3	BAILEY Ottis F	1		Dec		cholera infantum
4	VENABLES	1		Apr		whooping cough
5	BROWN William	1		Aug		cholera infantum
46	LLOYD Mary J	51	m	Apr	Keeping house	unknown
59	SEABREAZE Hester E	3		Jul		typhoid fever
63	EVANS William H	1		May		cholera infantum
79	ENGLISH John E	1		Jul		cholera infantum
90	GRAVENOR Margaret	65	m	May	Keeping house	pneumonia
129	WALKER Charles	60	m	Apr	Ship carpenter	pneumonia
149	COVINGTON John A	42	m	Nov	Shoe maker	pneumonia
151	JOHNSON Thomas J	35		Mch	Farmer	lung bleeding
151	JOHNSON Thomas C	79	m	Mch	Farmer	lung bleeding
166	BENNETT Nancy	72	m	Dec	Keeping house	lung bleeding
179	PIPPIN Roxanna	2		Apr		cholera infantum
211	BRADLEY Margaret a	1		Sep		cholera infantum
225	MILL Lemuel M	59	m	Feb	Farmer	stomach bleeding
240	McALISTER Samuel A	1		Mch		cholera infantum
244	BENNETT Edward J	1		Jul		cholera infantum
267	VINCENT John N	1		Aug		cholera infantum

12	COLLIER Maranda	51	m		Aug	Keeping house	pneumonia
44	PHILLIPS John B	5			Nov		dyspepsia
44	COLLIER Emma	17			Nov	Domestic	hemorrhage stomach
53	BAILEY Henry	1B			Apr		cholera infantum
55	PHILLIPS Anna	20	m		Jan	Keeping house	typhoid fever
77	BISHOP John	18B			Jun	Laborer	hemorrhage lungs
81	GILES Anna	1			Jun		cholera infantum
162	ALLEN Henry W	3B			Jun		typhoid fever
163	HANDY Leah	50B	m		Mch	Keeping house	hemorrhage lungs
163	HANDY Mintie	2B			Apr		cholera infantum
178	BRADLEY William	63	m		Mch	Ship Carpenter	hemorrhage lungs
233	LERICH Joseph E	46	m	De	Apr	Farmer	hemorrhage lungs
347	WALLER John W	1B			Jul		whooping cough

17	SCOTT Williams Anna	24	m	Feb	Keeping house
34	BREVINGTON Anna M	35	m	Aug	Keeping house
37	ELZEY George W	14B		Aug	Laborer
54	NECHER Elijah Thomas	1B		May	
157	WILLIAMS Mary	50	w	Jul	
197	PORTER Mary Anne	40	m	Jun	Keeping house
216	CODERRY Elizabeth	52	m	Mch	Keeping house
220	TILGHMAN Mary E	33	m	Nov	Keeping house
238	LARAMORE George R	35	m	Mch	Oysterman

249	NORTH William	65	w		Apr	Oysterman	ascites
263	HALEY James H	41	m		Jan	Blacksmith	chronic diarrhea
284	RIGGEN James C	3B			Mch		whooping cough
290	MOORE George	10			Apr		drowned
300	CHASE Julia A	1B			Mch		pneumonia
337	CONWAY Sarah	43M	m		Apr	Keeping house	typhoid fever
352	DASHIELL Emerson	1			Jul		typhoid fever
435	POLLETT Hester	44	w		Sep		chronic diarrhea

PITTSBURG DISTRICT - WICOMICO COUNTY 1870 -

33	LAYTON Mary C H	47	m		Jul	Keeping house	fever
34	LEWIS Isaac J	39	m		Aug	Farmer	brain disease
75	BETHRAS Joshua H	1			Feb		fever
76	PARSONS John R	17			Dec	Farmer	pleurisy
88	PRIDEAUX Gilly	74	m		Mch	Farmer	brain fever
100	STATON Harriet	1			Nov		dyptheria
134	BRITTINGHAM Jorden	1/12			Jan		diarrhea
148	SHEPPARD Hester	1B			Jul		diarrhea
150	SMITH Hester	50	m		Jul	Keeping house	consumption
169	DUNNAWAY Joseph	15			May	Farm hand	
177	SMITH Nathan	88	w		Apr	Farmer	old age
196	DUNNAWAY Charlotte	66	w		Jul	Keeping house	consumption
220	PARSONS Nolan	1/12			Feb		
273	WORKMAN William	1			Oct		
275	MELSON Alfred	6/12			May		cholera infantum
277	WEST Albert	1		De	Mch		cholera
308	BROWN George P	47			Feb	Farmer	pneumonia
348	DENNIS James	1/12			Dec		

DENNIS DISTRICT - WICOMICO COUNTY 1870

10	SMITH Margaret	50	m		Aug	Keeping house	dropsey
26	COLLINS Moses M	5			Mch		croup
93	BAILEY Nancy C	11/12			Nov		dropsey
98	PRIDEAUX Lemuel	11			Oct		dropsey

PARSONS DISTRICT - WICOMICO COUNTY 1870

8	KELLY James	65	w		May	Farmer	dropsey
13	DRASON Sallie	60	m		Nov	Keeping house	dyspepsia
25	DAVIS William J	5			Dec		dropsey
28	HOLLOWAY Daniel	1			Feb		scarlet fever
40	JOHNSON Rosabelle	7B			Sep		dyptheria
52	HILL Benjamin J	4			Sep		inflammation brain
58	PARSONS Phyllis	30B			May	Domestic	consumption
62	PARKER Edward	15			Feb	Farm worker	typhoid fever
108	HEARN Joseph	60	m		Aug	Farmer	liver disease
110	WHITE Minerva	20			Nov		inflammation stomach
115	HEARN Margaret	1			Aug		typhoid fever
118	BRITTINGHAM John	21			Jul	Farm worker	typhoid fever

124	SMITH Sarah D	43 m	May	Keeping house	consumption
129	HUDSON Wesley A	83	Sep		typhoid fever
141	PERDUE Rozena	5	Dec		croup
154	GORDY Lambert	46 m	Sep	Farmer	dropsey
154	GORDY Lemul H	11	Nov		dropsey
178	ADKINS Leah	50 m	Jun		dropsey

UPPER TRAPPE DISTRICT - WICOMICO COUNTY 1870

1	JACKSON Messie E	2	May		colic
14	COTMAN --	70B m	Jan	Laborer	hemorrhage stomach
21	NOBLE Eliza A	29B m	Aug	Keeping house	hemorrhage stomach
45	BREVINGTON Isaac	1B	May		whooping cough
57	MALONE Allena	1	Jul		dyspepsia
59	DENSON William	2	May		cholera infantum
115	JONES --	1	Mch		cholera infantum
129	STEPHENS James	60 m	Dec	Farmer	burned
130	COTMAN Levin G	4B	Dec		dyptheria
140	TAYLOR William	79 m	Feb	Laborer	hemorrhage stomach
146	WHITE Beachamp	50 m	Jul	Farmer	paralysis
225	POLLETT Anne	60B m	Jul	Keeping house	hemorrhage stomach
230	RIGGENS Geniva E	1	Aug		cholera infantum
236	RHINE Martha E	1	Sep		cholera infantum

NUTTERS DISTRICT - WICOMICO COUNTY 1870

2	FOOKS Olivia B	1B	Apr		whooping cough
7	NIBLETT William L	36 m	Jun	Day laborer	kidney disease
8	MORRIS Martha F	37 m	May	Keeping house	consumption
8	MORRIS Martha A	2/12	Jul		consumption
9	SMULLEN Etta	6/12	May		cholera infantum
46	OWINGS Martha	2	Jun		dyptheria
60	GORDY Mary	21	Aug		typhoid fever
77	CATHELL Levin	1	Aug		whooping cough
83	DICKERSON John	1/12	Sep		unknown
83	DICKERSON James	1/12	Sep		
88	HUMPHRIES Comfort	30B m	May	Keeping house	dropsey
99	DUKES Lafayette	3	Oct		dyptheria
108	GRAY William	4	May		typhoid fever
113	McALISTER Jesse	80 w	Mch	Miller	old age
123	FOOKS Anna L	7	Feb		croup
125	SHOCKLEY Belle	7	Feb		dyptheria
129	WINBROW Julia	59 m	Apr	Keeping house	pneumonia
150	DYKES Jefferson L	7	Sep		dyptheria
150	DYKES Ellen	4	Sep		dyptheria
150	DYKES Marion	1	Sep		dyptheria
151	PRIOR William	2/12	Feb		whooping cough

19	WHITE Alpheus	1		Jul		croup
19	TINDLE Ann	23B		Jul	Domestic	dropsey
21	CATHELL Emma	2		May		measles
84	HUSTON John	1B		Oct		fall
104	WALSTON Edward	2		Aug		measles
110	CATHELL Rosa F	33 m		Jun	Keeping house	remittant fever
127	FARLOW John T	1		Jul		cholera infantum
137	WHITE William W	3		Jul		spine disease
146	SMITH William H	2/12		May		whooping cough
149	BENNETT Nancy	55 m		Nov	Keeping house	pneumonia
150	HARRINGTON Ellen	25		Apr		consumption
155	ADAMS Eglantine	43 m	De	Aug		remittant fever
157	RIDER Edward	18B		Aug	Sailor	heart disease
172	WILSON Sallie	18B		May	Domestic	consumption
173	DUKES Helen	7/12		Jul		cholera infantum
175	GRANT Ulysses S	7		Mch		whooping cough
178	AIKMAN William	79 m		Dec	Painter	consumption
245	COTTMAN George	85B m		Jan	Laborer	general debility
256	HOOPER Thomas F	13		Jul		typhoid fever
263	JASMINE Thomas B	1		Mch		whooping cough
264	JUDAH Charles D	46 m		Feb	Lawyer	apoplexy
278	WILLIAMS Jennie M	2		Mch		whooping cough
279	MILLS James E	2		May		laryngitis
281	HORSEY Charles	80 m		Jul	Farmer	consumption
311	MESSIER Samuel E	1B		Jan		cholera infantum
314	CROUCH Sallie	84 w		Feb	Keeping house	heart disease
333	STILLMAN George	40 m	De	Dec	Keeping house	erysipelas
335	COLLIER Stephen B	57 m	De	Jul	Blacksmith	heart disease
354	CANNON George	1		Jun		diarrhea
363	PRIOR Hester	68		Aug	House keeper	dysentary
366	DICKERSON Mary	28		Sep	Keeping house	consumption
366	DICKERSON Mary	2/12		Nov		consumption
379	FASSITT Margaret	45B m		Jun	Keeping house	consumption
383	BEAUCHAMP Virginia	1		Oct		erysipelas
392	WINDSOR Nancy	1/12		Aug		remittant fever
404	CANTWELL George H	3		Jul		acute dysentary
404	CANTWELL John	4/12		Nov		croup

	SALISBURY DISTRICT - WICOMICO COUNTY 1870					
10	STEMONS Louisa	1		Jun		hydrocephalus
29	HASTINGS Willis	3/12		Jul		cholera infantum
43	FOWLER Amelia H	34 m		Aug	Keeping house	consumption
43	JOHNSON Thomas Jr	36		Mch	Farm worker	cut by circular saw
43	JOHNSON Thomas Sr	78 m		Mch	Farmer	old age
51	WALLER Ann	3/12		Feb		consumption
57	HEARN Thoamona	1/12		Jul		cholera infantum

8	HENDERSON George	3/12		Aug		dysentary
22	HALL Annie	14		Feb	school	diptheria
32	CLARK Thomas	5		Feb		diptheria
32	CLARK Otha	3		May		diptheria
42	VICTOR Minie	1		May		diptheria
22	HALL Archibald	1		Feb		dysentary
43	STUCKLEY Joshua	75B m		Dec	Farmer	consumption
43	MARSHALL Cordelia	4/12B		Mch		croup
48	BERRY Henrietta	49M m		Jun		consumption
60	BROADANTER Levin	61 m	Va	Sep	Hotel keeper	paralysis
63	CRISP Andrew	36 m	Pa	Sep	work saw mill	accidentally killed
64	FOOKS Sallie	39B m		Apr		consumption
65	DENNIS Annie	1B		Aug		brain fever
65	QUINN Alice	3/12B		Sep		croup
74	TOWNSEND Christian	1		Jan		pneumonia
75	BRITINGHAM Jane	30B w		Sep		died from whipping
80	HITCH James	2/12		Jul		inflammation brain
86	BRITINGHAM Cora L	1		May		cholera infantum
87	BRAVIS Sarah	2/12		Nov		pneumonia
89	KITCHENS Hannah	30B m		Feb		kidney disease
92	WHITINGTON John	18B		Apr	Laborer	drowned
97	HEARN Sarah	5B		Feb		drowned
97	RUSH Georgia	1B		Jul		measles
99	BALLARD John	1/12B		Sep		cholera infantum
121	SATONIUS Josephine	4	Va ffb	Nov		diabetes
144	JONES Birde	1		Feb		congestive chills
151	BROUGHTON Mary	38 m		Nov	Keeping house	consumption
151	McCRADY Alfred	13B		Jan		dropsey
154	FALKNER William	6/12		Jul		acute dysentary
157	DASHIELDS Charlotte	35 m		Mch	Keeping house	pneumonia
164	BALL Samuel	50 m		Mch	Farmer	consumption
175	HENRY Minie	1B		Aug		diarrhea
183	POWELL Earnest	5/12		Jul		brain disease
198	MERRILL William C	72 m		Mch	Ret merchant	consumption
200	MILLS Leah	77 w		Jul	Lady	consumption
201	QUINN Sallie	27 m		Sep	Lady	typhoid fever
201	QUINN Sallie	1/12		Sep		typhoid fever
205	HAT John	3/12B		Jan		croup
207	SCHOOLFIELD Sabre	72B m		Apr		consumption
219	PAYNE Pierson	7		Sep		remittant fever
256	CONQUEST Ellen	14B	Va	Jul		remittant fever
256	CONQUEST Philace	1/12B		Aug		thrush
257	AYDELOTTE Oliver	20		May	Laborer	consumption
260	JOHNSON Mary	2/12		May		whooping cough
263	WATSON Sarah	4		Nov		fever
263	WATSON Mary	2		Sep		fever
268	JONES Mary	15B m		Aug		consumption
268	JONES Julia	2B		Aug		croup
269	PHILLIPS Catharine	41 m		Jan	Keeping house	consumption

274	HAYWARD Sarah	12B		Feb		consumption
274	HAYWARD George	1/12B		Nov		croup
272	MELVIN Kate	78 w	Va	Jun		consumption
289	POWELL Ida	1		Mch		typhoid fever
311	OVERLY Charles	50B m		Jan	Waterman	dropsey
323	ROBINS Sarah	40B m		Sep		child birth
331	COLBOURNE George	1/12B		Sep		croup
336	HENDERSON Noah	79 m		Jun	Farmer	erysipelis
337	RICHARDSON Ida	3/12		Aug		cholera infantum
341	WATERS Sophia	5		May		drowned
348	BOSTON Ina	1B		May		diarrhea
355	BOSTON Hiram	3B		Apr		measles
360	WHITE John	1/12B		Apr		thrush
361	POWELL Sabre	72B m		Apr		consumption
372	DENNIS Polly	26B		May		hemorrhage lungs
373	HENDERSON Annie	17		May		consumption
375	COLLINS Robert	1B		Jul		typhoid
385	BROWN Sarah	1/12B		May		thrush
386	CONNER Pamela	32 m	Va	May	Keeping house	consumption
388	MASON Ann	50B m		May	Keeping house	childbirth
409	SELBY Jane	12B		Jul		diarrhea
409	SELBY Sidney	10B		Sep		diarrhea
411	DENNIS Jane	11B		Jul		consumption
411	DENNIS Sidney	9B		Jun		typhoid fever
435	SCOTT Joseph	50		Sep		dropsey
438	STEVENSON Hill	70B w		Sep		intermittant fever
451	WISE James	22B w		Jun	Farmer	typhoid fever
451	WISE Oliver	17B		Mch	Waterman	consumption
456	MATTHEWS James	1		Oct		whooping cough
490	HENDERSON Charles	2		May		croup
504	MASON Ida	2		Jun		diptheria
506	BOSTON Evan	80 w		Aug		consumption
511	MULLETT Susan	3		Aug		intermittant fever

DISTRICT #2 - WORCESTER COUNTY 1870

263	BLAKE Polly	90 w		Sep	Keeping house	consumption
285	BOWDEN Harriet	50 m		Mch	Keeping house	remittent fever
291	CLAYVILLE Annie	16		Dec	Domestic	diptheria
291	ROWLEY David	6/12		Jan		diptheria
296	SPRUCE George	60		Jul	Waterman	consumption
296	ROBINS James B	31 m		Jan	Farmer	heart disease
316	HOLLAND Levin	4B		Mch		bowel disease
316	SHOWELL George	5/12B		Mch		croup
333	RICHARDSON John	2/12B		Jan		bowel disease
353	RILEY Mary	24 m		May	Keeping house	childbirth
357	AYDELOTTE Isabelle	4		Jun		diptheria
357	CLAYVILLE Annie	16		Dec		diptheria
363	RICHARDSON Benjamin	45 w		Dec	Waterman	consumption

378	GUTHARIE Thomas	9		Dec		diptheria
378	GUTHARIE Laura	3		Dec		diptheria
378	GUTHARIE Elmira	6		Dec		diptheria
379	TRUITT Maggie	7		Jun		diptheria
379	TRUITT George	6		Jun		diptheria
379	TRUITT CLARA	11		Jun		diptheria
379	TRUITT Charles	3		Jun		diptheria
391	BISHOP George	6B		Apr		measles
398	MERRITT Isaac	37	m	Oct	Waterman	typhoid fever
404	POWELL Henry	6		Oct		remittant fever
408	BRATTEN William	6B		Apr		measles
423	NICHOLSON Irene	6		Apr		measles
424	HARMAN Nancy	17B		Dec	Keeping house	intermittant fever
429	HADOCK James	72	m	Oct		remittant fever
431	HARMAN Nice	18B		Dec		diptheria
443	CROPPER John	70		Feb		disease of lungs
"	RICHARDSON William	60		Jan		intermittant fever
"	HARTHWAY James	45		Feb		dropsey
"	MARSHALL Maria	1		Mch		bowel disease
"	BEAVINS Cole	100B	w	Feb		leg sores
"	N____ Peregaw	100B	w	Feb		leg soresm
"	MORRIS John	45B	m	May		rheumatism
443	PITTS George	80B		Mch		consumption
"	JOHNSON George	79B		Sep		heart disease
"	SPRUCE Rufus	55B	w	Jun		lung disease
"	SHELLY Nelly	170B	w	Oct		remittant fever
"	BIRD Julia	16B		Jun		dropsey
"	BROWN Jane	13B		May		dropsey
451	PURNELL George	4B		Sep		bowel disease
462	DALE Elizabeth	60	m	May		insanity
484	ROBERTS William	21B		Jun	Farm worker	consumption
490	TAYLOR Jennie	1		Jun		bowel disease
491	HAT Caroline	1M		Oct		worms

DISTRICT # 2 - WORCESTER COUNTY 1870						
3	DRYDEN Littleton	30	m	Apr	Farmer	pneumonia
11	CLAYVILLE Lucy	1/12		Apr		fall/unknown
18	SPRUCE Irving	8/12B		May		diarrhea
39	NELSON Thomas	70		Feb	Farmer	cancer
44	SELBY John	1/12B		May		croup
50	WILSON Washington	1/12		May		bowel disease
53	HACK Mary	1		Jul		remittant fever
55	SPRUCE Jennie	1		Jul		convulsions
57	TAYLOR george	21		Jan	Store clerk	consumption
59	COLLINS William	19		Aug	at school	consumption
60	PORTER Lule	2		Dec		intermittant fever
71	ROUND Henry	23B		May	Waterman	consumption
88	VICKERS Laura	30	m	Apr	Keeping house	consumption

90	JONES Henry	2B		Jun		lung disease
94	PURNELL Annie	42 m		Aug	Keeping house	rheumatism
105	CORDREY Frank	1		Dec		dysentary
107	CLAYVILLE William	1		Dec		whooping cough
109	PURNELL George	23B		Jan	Farmer	consumption
112	BAILY Stephen	1B		Obt		cholera infantum
116	PURNELL John	1B		Jul		croup
126	KEAS William	1		Sep		cholera infantum
130	SMITH Edward	65B m		Jul	Farmer	consumption
155	CORBIN John	24B m		May	Laborer	consumption
155	CARTER Peter	70B m		Jul	Farmer	consumption
166	DALE William	10/12B		Jul		croup
167	IRVING Annie	6		Jul		quinsy/tonsilitis
167	IRVING John	1/12		Nov		fall/unknown
191	ALLEN Levin	100B w		Oct	Laborer	consumption
197	PHILLIPS Mary	1B		Mch		diptheria
198	MARSHALL Georgia	9/12B		Aug		inflammation brain
202	WATERS Elizabeth	85 w		Sep	Keeping house	consumption
209	BRATTEN Esther	65B m		Apr	Keeping house	hemorrhage lung
214	HANDY John	45B m		Aug	Laborer	drowned
220	DAFFIELD Albert	1/12B		May		bowel disease
262	JOHNSON Edward	20		Mch	Waterman	remittant fever

DISTRICT #6 - WORCESTER COUNTY 1870

1	BRERETON James	59 m		Jan	Farmer	dropsey
4	McKEE Georgiana	1/12		Oct		bowel disease
6	MUMFORD James	1		Jul		typhoid fever
11	KIRKE Thomas	25		May	Laborer	diptheria
26	SHOCKLEY Christiana	1/12		Oct		diptheris
49	FIGGS George	3/12		Feb		diptheria
59	HAPMAN Martha	5		Sep		measles
64	STRAUGHN Maggie	3/12		Feb		croup
64	STRAUGHN Eliza	1/12		Apr		croup
78	WILKENS John	5		Aug		brain disease
102	COLBORNE John	30		Mch	Farm worker	consumption
104	BELLE Ross	8		May		diptheria
115	MUMFORD James	70 m		Jan	Farmer	kidney disease
117	GODFREY Eugene	3		Aug		diptheria
124	MORTON Mary	12B		Mch		diptheria
125	EVANS Charles	1/12B		Mch		croup
145	TOWNSEND Jane	24B		Aug	Keeping house	typhoid fever
147	HUDSON James	2B		May		dropsey
150	HAYWARD Arthur	70 m		Jul	Laborer	dropsey

DISTRICT #7 - WORCESTER COUNTY 1870

7	TOWNSEND Tayle	69 m		Oct	Farmer	
30	STAGG Mary	1/12		Oct		
38	SCHOOLFIELD Jennie	1/12		Sep		
69	PUSEY Martha	24 m		Apr	Keeping house	

75	FLEMING Mary	1/12	May		bowel disease
85	PUSEY Cora	1/12	Aug		bowel disease
106	BEAVIS Robert	3/12	Mch		bowel disease
119	RUARK Annie	3	Jul		remittant fever
120	ATKINSON Amelia	2B	May		remittant fever
125	FLEMING William	2B	Jul		bowel disease
143	TAYLOR george	1/12	Feb		fall/unknown
148	MADDOX William	2B	May		bowel disease
157	BRUMBLY George	1/12	Feb		bowel disease
167	BEAUCHAMP John	1/12	Sep		bowel disease
170	RUARK George	3	Aug		remittant fever
191	WILSON Mary	60 w	Jun	Keeping house	apoplexy
208	BROWN George	1/12	Mch		bowel disease
214	JOHNSON John	45B m	Apr	Farmer	intermittant fever
225	MADDOX James	4/12	May		croup
241	CONNER John	2B	May		inflammation brain

	DISTRICT #8 - WORCESTER COUNTY	1870			
11	SELBY Mary E	11	Nov	at school	scarlet fever
34	HANCOCK Harriet	29 m	Dec	Keeping house	consumption
44	____ Kelly	16	Jul		typhoid fever
35	TARR Ann	29	Aug		typhoid fever
70	SELBY Henry	1B	Jun		convulsions
76	SCARBOROUGH Peter	67 m	Jun	Farmer	acute diarrhea
124	HUDSON Sallie	64 m	Feb	Keeping house	consumption
140	TAYLOR Elizabeth	44 m	Feb	Keeping house	intermittant fever
152	TILGHMAN William	1/12	Oct		croup
155	HANCOCK William	1/12	Oct		croup
156	COLLINS William	19	Oct		inflammation brain
158	LINDSAY George W	27 w	Aug	Farmer	consumption
159	HANCOCK Annie	8	Jun	at school	inflammation bowel
164	REDDEN Ina	2/12	Jul		thrush
171	HARRISON George	2/12B	Sep		thrush
182	COLLICK John	11M	Jun		dropsey
182	COLLICK Eda	18M	Jul		consumption
184	CHAPMAN John	7	Sep		typhoid fever
184	CHAPMAN William	1	May		whooping cough
185	MANUEL Benjamin	2B	Dec		dropsey
188	REDDEN Stephen	85M w	Oct	Farmer	typhoid fever
188	FOSKY Moses	36B m	Oct	Farmer	typhoid fever
192	COLLINS Irving	25B m	May	Farmer	consumption
195	HANCOCK Major	7/12	Jul		chronic diarrhea
201	FIELDS Grant	1/12B	Apr		croup
208	ALLEN Edward	75B	Oct		inflammation legs
214	MITCHEL Annie	56 m	Oct	Keeping house	dropsey
215	ALLEN Sallie	22b m	Dec	Keeping house	childbirth
225	LINDSAY Moses	11B	May	Farm worker	drowned
225	LINDSAY Lemuel	36B m	Aug	Farm worker	consumption

227	HAUBERT Levi	4		Sep		dropsey
231	DENNIS Ellen	1/12B		Aug		croup
248	PARADISE Nancy	85	w	Jan		consumption
250	JONES Georgia	1/12		Jan		croup
257	FIELDS Caroline	28B	m	Apr	Domestic	consumption
259	WATSON Polly	74	w	Nov		dropsey
259	WATSON Henry	3		Nov		jaundice
261	CORBIN Peter	50	m	Jun	Farmer	murdered/shot
291	MANUEL John	3B		Apr		rickets
293	HOLLAND James	6/12B		Mch		dysentary
300	SELBY Ellen	1B		Dec		croup
300	SELBY Annie	2B		Jul		croup
329	TULL Gideon	36	m	Oct	Farmer	typhoid
344	WHEALTON Samuel	2B		Aug		fractured back
363	CORTON John	20		Apr	Farmer	bronchitis
369	WATSON West	83	m	Aug	Farmer	consumption
380	HARTHWAY Levin	11		Oct		fever
383	COLLINS Ellen	2B		Jan		croup
394	SELBY Leah	1B		May		convulsions
398	DUKES Levinia	1/12		May		croup

INDEX

BURTON - 12,31
BUSH - 23
BUSICK - 19
BUTLER - 4,16
BUTTER - 19
BYUS - 12

C ___ - 1,16
CALEB - 5
CALLAHAN - 38
CAMP - 17,19
CAMPBELL - 34
CAMPER - 12,13,23
CANEY - 45
CANNON - 3,29,43
CANTWELL - 43
CARLISLE - 1
CARNE - 30
CARPENTER - 35
CARROL - 33,35
CARTER - 49
CATHELL - 42,43,45
CATHERS - 7
CATSCOTT - 33
CAULK - 17,35,39
CAUSEY - 2
CEPHAS - 9,10,14,15
CHAMBERLAIN - 34
CHAMBERS - 19,21
CHANCE - 24,36
CHANDLER - 8
CHANEY - 35
CHAPMAN - 25,50
CHARLES - 9
CHASE - 14,21,35,41
CHESTER - 11,13
CHETAN - 27
CHEW - 23
CHRISTOPHER - 38
CHUZMAN - 34
CLARK - 1,18,37,45,46
CLAYTON - 17,33
CLAYVILLE - 47,48,49
CLEMONS - 5
COCTON - 45,47
CODERRY - 40,49
COFFIN - 45
COLEMAN - 10
COLGAN - 25
COLLICK - 50
COLLIER - 40,43
COLLINS - 2,9,20,31,41,47,48
         50,51
COLLISON 9,34
COMEGYS - 19,23,25
CONADEN - 24
CONNER - 28,47,50
CONNOLLY - 1,3,25,33,44

CONQUEST - 46
CONWAY - 9,41
CONYER - 26
COOK - 3,5,7,12
COOLING - 6
COONEY - 34
COOPER - 9,25,27,33,35,39,44
CORBIN - 49,51
CORDREY - 49
CORK - 18
CORKRAN - 15
CORNISH - 9,12,13,15,36
CORTON - 51
COTMAN - 42,43
COULBORN - 2,28,30,47,49
COUNCIL - 24
COVEY - 36,38
COVINGTON - 40
COX - 30,44
CRAMER - 6
CRAWFORD - 6
CREADINE - 26
CREIGHTON - 13
CRESWELL - 5
CRISP - 29,46
CROCKET - 27,37
CROMWELL - 13
CROPPER - 45,48
CROSBY - 4
CROSS - 33
CROSSLEY - 18
CROUCH - 43
CROUSE - 7
CROWELL - 30
CULLEN - 27
CUMMING - 39
CUNNINGHAM - 6
CURTIS - 28,30,31
CURRY - 5

DAFFIELD - 49
DALE - 27,35,48,49
DARBY - 29
DASHIELL - 27,41,44,46
DAUGHERTY - 31
DAVIDSON - 26
DAVIS - 2,4,6,7,9,10,13,15,16,17
        19,21,26,28,29,37,41,45
DAWSON - 15,26
DEAN - 2,5,10
DEFORD - 24
DELL - 24
DELLAHAY - 26
DEMMING - 34
DENNIS - 27,41,45,46,47,51
DENNY - 19,34
DENSON - 42
DENWOOD - 10

GRANGER - 20
GRAVENOR - 40
GRAY - 42,45
GREEN(E) - 1,33,34,35,38
GREENWOOD - 20
GREGG - 8
GRIFFIN - 11,15,26,31,33,37,45
GRIFFITH - 2
GURDY - 5
GUTHRIE - 4,48

H___ - 29
HACK - 48
HACKET - 14,20,24
HADAWAY - 39
HADOCK - 48
HAGUE - 18
HAINES - 8
HALEY - 41
HALL - 30,46
HAMBLETON - 36
HAMMON(D) - 4,5
HAMSLEY - 37
HANCOCK - 50
HANDY - 15,25,27,30,36,40,49
HANES -20
HANSON - 20
HAPMAN - 49
HARDCASTLE - 37
HARGIS - 29,46
HARMON - 14,48
HARPER - 10
HARRIMAN - 7
HARRINGTON - 13,36,43
HARRIS - 8,25,29,31,32
HARRISON - 35,36,39,50
HART - 6
HARTHWAY - 48,51
HARTLEY - 23
HARVEY - 7,30
HASSET - 38
HASTINGS - 27,43,45
HAT(TE) - 45,46,48
HAUBERT - 51
HAYES - 4,21
HAYMAN - 27
HAYWARD - 29,30,47,49
HAZELTON - 25
HEARN - 41,43,46
HEATH - 6,15,26,27
HEMPHIL - 4
HEMPHREY - 17
HENDERSON - 46,47
HENNESSE - 36
HENRY - 10,24,25,34,45,46
HERBERT - 25
HICKMAN - 27

HICKS - 13
HIGGENS - 26
HILL - 12,41
HINSON,HYNSON - 20,23,25
HITCH - 27,46
HOBBS - 9,35,36
HODGSON - 18
HOLDEN - 18,24
HOLLAND - 15,29,47,51
HOLLIDAY - 14,19,36
HOLLIS - 10
HOLLOW - 10
HOLLOWAY - 41
HOLLY - 19,20
HOLTON - 5
HOOPER - 13,43
HOPKINS - 21
HORSEMAN - 14
HORSEY - 28,43
HOUSTON - 38,43
HOWARD - 28
HOWETH - 9,28
HUBBARD - 2,12
HUDSON - 42,45,49,50
HUETT - 33
HUGH - 1
HUGHES - 15,34
HUGHLETT - 36
HULL - 28,30
HUMAN - 14
HUMPHRIES - 42
HUTCHENS - 25

INSLEY - 11
IRELAND - 39
IRSLETON - 26
IRVING - 49
IRWIN - 7

JACKSON - 8,14,21,33,34,35,42
JACOBS - 25
JAMES - 3,37
JANNEY - 5
JARRETT - 24
JARVIS - 45
JASMINE - 43
JEFFERSON - 37
JENKINS - 14,36
JESTER - 3,36
JOHNS - 9,17,25
JOHNSON - 5,9,10,14,16,18,19,21,
         24,26,27,28,30,31,33,38,
         40,41,43,46,48,49,50
JONES - 4,11,12,18,19,20,21,24,27
        28,33,42,46,49,51
JOPP - 2
JOSHUA - 9
JUDAH - 43

KEARSEY - 28
KEAS - 49
KEENE - 11,12,13,14
KELLY - 24,25,28,38,41,45
KEMP - 1,2
KENNARD - 34
KENNEDY - 21
KENNY - 10
KERNS - 7
KIAH - 14
KILLMON - 15,35
KIMBLE - 7
KING - 27
KINNEMON - 39
KIRBY - 36,38
KIRE - 13
KIRK - 6,7,35,49
KIRWAN - 11
KITCHENS - 46
KITE - 29
KNIGHT - 8,16
KNOX - 17

LACY - 24
LAMBDEN - 29
LAMBERT - 1
LANDON - 30
LANE - 14,24,34
LANG - 2
LANGHARTY - 31
LANKFORD - 28,31
LARDNER - 6
LARRIMORE - 35,40
LATON - 23
LAWRENCE - 7,18,34
LAWSON - 31
LAYTON -41
LEATHERBERRY - 30
LEE - 9,12,39,44
LEGG - 25
LEMERICK - 24
LEMON - 4
LEONARD - 35
LERICK - 40
LEWIS - 1,41
LINDSAY - 50
LINTHICUM - 12,13
LINTON - 8
LLOYD - 34,40
LOGAN - 15
LONG - 30
LORD - 10,28
LOVE - 5
LOVEDAY - 34
LOWARY - 39
LOWE - 9,12,39,44
LUCAS - 1,38
LYNCH - 5,25
LYONS - 10

M_LLY - 23
MACER - 13
MACKEY - 4,24,36
MADDOX - 22,30,50
MAGDELINA - 29
MAGNAN - 7
MAHAN - 4
MAHANNEY -7
MALONE - 42
MALOY - 25
MANAKY - 34
MANDEN - 18
MANDRILL - 33
MANN - 17
MANSFIELD - 1,26
MANUEL - 50,51
MARINE - 9
MARKEY - 17
MARSH - 30
MARSHALL - 12,27,35,39,46,48,49
MARTIN - 16,17,37
MA(Y)SON - 11,17,31,47
MATHEWS - 18,28,29,34,36,38,47
McALLISTER - 10,27,40,42
McBEY - 5
McCALLOUGH - 5
McCAULEY - 5,17
McCLANAHAN - 7
McCONIGAN - 38
McCRADY - 46
McCULLOUGH - 7
McDANIEL - 4
McDOUGLE - 6
McFARLAND - 1
McGRATH - 9,27
McGUIRE - 17
McHAILL - 31
McKEE - 49
McKENNY,McKINNEY - 5,7,17
McMARTIN - 8
McNAB - 45
McNAMARA - 1
McNATT - 17
McNEAL - 4
McQUAY - 38
McVEY -7
MEADY - 25
MEARS - 22
MEDFORD - 19
MEEKINS - 13,20
MELLY - 35
MELSON - 41
MELVIN - 35,47
MEREDITH - 14,15,26
MERRICK - 23,36
MERRILL - 46
MERRITT - 20,48
MESSEX - 37
MILBOURNE - 29

MILES - 13,29,30,31
MILLA - 29
MILLER - 1,2,17,25,36
MILLS - 40,46
MINNER - 39
MINUS - 37
MISTER - 30,31
MITCHELL - 8,50
MOBRAY - 12,13
MOFFETT - 18,24
MOLOCK - 14
MOONEY - 10
MOORE - 7,10,11,12,15,36,41,44
MORGAN - 24,38
MORRELL - 6
MORRIS - 6,18,42,48
MORRISON - 6,7
MORTON - 17,49
MOSS - 19
MUIR - 31
MULLUTT - 47
MULLIKEN - 35,37
MUMFORD - 49
MUNSON - 20
MURPHY - 6,9,10
MURRAY - 5,8,20,34
MURREL - 29
MYERS - 4,36

NANCE - 17
NEAL - 14
NECKER - 40
NEELY - 39
NEIGHBORS - 38
NELSON - 27,31
NESBITT - 6,9
NEWMAN - 27,27,35,36
NEWNAM - 37
NEWTON - 17
NIBLETT - 42
NICHOLAS - 45
NICHOLS - 3,34,37
NICHOLSON - 19,20,26,44,48
NICKERSON - 18
NICOLS - 10
NOBLE - 42
NORRIS - 4
NORTH - 12,41
NOTLEY - 7
NUMBERS - 17

OREM - 35
OTHER - 13
OUTEN - 1,28,29
OVERLY - 47
OWENS - 20
OWINGS - 42

PALMER - 4,13,35
PARADISE - 51
PARDEE - 23
PARKER - 2,9,13,27,33,41
PARKS - 13
PARMER - 5,38,39
PARROTT - 37,38
PARSONS - 14,41,45
PASTERFIELD - 36
PATTERSON - 27,28
PAXSON - 8
PAYNE - 46
PEARCE - 20,21
PEARSON - 1
PEEKER - 17
PEOPLES - 7
PERDUE - 42
PERKINS - 4,38
PETERS - 45
PHABRIA - 28
PHILLIPS - 6,8,40,44,46,49
PHYSIC - 8
PIERSON - 4
PIKER - 24
PINDER - 11
PIPPIN - 40
PITTS - 48
PLATER - 23,38
PLUMMER - 33
POLLETT,POLLIT - 27,41,42
PORTER - 18,27,40,48
POTTER - 34
POWELL - 45,46,47,48
PRATT - 23
PRICE - 16,17,23,24,31,36
PRICHHEAD - 44
PRIDEAUX - 41
PRIOR - 42,43
PRITCHETT - 13,14
PURNELL - 4,45,48,49
PUSEY - 27,49

QUIMBY - 38
QUINN - 46

R___ - 16
RAISIN 17,10,20,21
RAWLEIGH - 10
RAY - 33
REAGAN - 12
REALLY - 19
REDDEN - 50
REDDITT - 12
REDMAN - 38
REED - 9,19,31,37
REEDER - 5,7
REESE - 30

SUTTON - 16,17,33
SWIFT - 29

TAN - 36
TANNER - 19
TARAS - 31
TARBUTTON - 35,38
TARLOW - 28
TARR - 50
TAYLOR - 8,20,25,42,44,48,50
TEAT - 16
TERRY - 6
THOMAS - 4,5,7,12,14,17,18,21
        24,25,26,31,32,35,36,38
THOMPSON - 8,17,19,21,35
TILGHMAN - 24,27,40,50
TILLMAN - 7,10,21
TINDLE - 43
TODD - 11,12
TOLLY - 13
TOLSON - 25
TOWERS - 33
TOWNS - 2
TOWNSEND - 23,47,49
TRAVERS - 13,15,23
TREXLER - 11
TRICE - 2
TRUITT - 48
TUBMAN - 14
TUCKER - 5
TULL - 9,51
TURNER - 1,18,21,23
TURPEN - 28
TYLER - 11,13,27,31
TYSON - 6

VALIANT - 35,37
VANSANT - 18,24
VENABLES - 40,44
VICKERS - 48
VICTOR - 46
VINCENT - 40
VINEY - 33
VINSINGER - 5
VOSS - 20

W___ - 2
WACKETT - 17
WAINWRIGHT - 9
WALKER - 30,40
WALLACE - 9,11,28,31,37
WALLEN - 23
WALLER - 28,40,43
WALLS - 23
WALSH - 13
WALSTON - 43
WALTER - 23
WARD - 12,31
WARNER - 37,38

WARREN - 19,28,37
WASHINGTON - 30
WATERS - 10,3,0,47,49
WATKINS - 26
WATSON - 46,51
WAYMAN - 35
WAETHERLY - 44
WEBB - 10
WEBSTER - 2,29,32
WELLS - 13,24,25
WENTWORTH - 2
WEST - 41
WHEALTON - 35,46
WHEAT - 19
WHEATLEY - 9
WHEATON - 35
WHEELER - 2
WHIMBLE - 4
WHITE - 26,28,31,41,42,43,47
WHITTINGTON - 18,28,46
WIGGENS - 18
WILKENS - 28,29,49
WILKERSON - 1
WILKINSON - 18
WILLEY - 10,11,13
WILLIAMS - 1,21,25,29,34,38,40
          43,44
WILLIS - 2,5,37
WILLOUGHBY - 9,10
WILMER - 17
WILMORE - 17
WILSON - 1,3,4,6,8,10,14,17,18,
         19,21,25,29,30,34,38,43,
         48,50
WINBROW - 42
WINDSOR - 31,43
WINGATE - 10,12
WISE - 45,47
WOLF - 4
WOOD - 2
WOODLAND - 18,21,23
WOOLENS - 5,33
WOOLFORD - 12,13,38
WOOTERS - 2
WORDELL 4
WORK - 5
WORKMAN - 41
WORMEL - 20
WRIGHT - 9,14,15,18,19,20,24,31,
         38
WRIGHTSON - 14,34,39
WROTEN - 11,14
WYATT - 30

Y___ - 21
YOUNG - 10,13,14,15,34,37

Printed by
THE ANUNDSEN PUBLISHING CO.
108 Washington Street
Decorah, Iowa 52101